HEAVEN HELP US, NOW!

A Self-Help Guide to God's Own First
Responder, St. Jude Thaddeus

By Séamus Ó Fianghusa (Fennessy)

Im Úr Blasta

Published by Im Úr Blasta, LLC.
Old Bridge, NJ.

Library of Congress Control Number: 2021905987

ISBN 978-1-7369229-2-7 (hardcover)
ISBN 978-1-7369229-1-0 (paperback)
ISBN 978-1-7369229-0-3 (ebook)

Cover art by Pixel Clan
Art direction by Séamus Ó Fianghusa (Fennessy)
Cover image based on mosaic icon of St. Jude Thaddeus, Virgin Mary
Melkite Catholic Church, Brooklyn, NY

www.imurblasta.com

Do Phapa,
An tÚdar É Féin,
Ag coimheád ar a shaothar
Ó Shuaimhneas na bhFlaitheas

Acknowledgments

I am afraid that any attempt to fully name all those to whom I owe my success would require a book of its own. But I would be remiss if I did not at least make an attempt to identify some of the culprits.

I undertook this project acutely aware of the debt I owe to the generations of my lineage that preceded me. Without the thoroughly Celtic and Christian values of my kin, the Clann Fianghusa, I would be nothing and have nothing to pass on. Outside of my family, these values are most tangibly embodied in my brothers of the 69th Infantry, the Fighting Irish of New York. I also carry with me the combat lessons I learned with my brothers of the Mountain Cavalry of Vermont's Green Mountain Boys. "Scouts Out, Fág an Bealach!"

The wider Fennessy family has always been a powerful network of loyalty and love. My uncles have always shown themselves to be the essence of manhood. My aunts, and my Nana, and Gigi have been the heroines of my life. Endless love to them all. I thank my mother, the first human I bonded with. I thank my father, who more than anybody alive planted in me the love of God, family, and country. I thank my little sisters Mary Helen and Aileen, my first lessons in responsibility, always supportive, always loving.

To those of my family who rest in blessed repose and eternal memory, I am grateful beyond words. My Papa, to whom *Heaven Help*

Us, Now! is dedicated, was the author of an eternal legacy. My dear (great) Aunt Margie, a bride of Christ – her kindness was legendary and her influence profound. And I keep always before me my three children, three sons, who never made it to birth but who preceded me in getting to where I want to go. In so many visible and invisible ways they guide and guard me, their mother, and their sisters.

My stepdaughter Olivia, affectionately known as Blast; she has given me much spiritual food for thought, for which I thank her. I give my heartfelt thanks and love to my wife Deirdre – our amazing journey together brought St. Jude Thaddeus into our lives, and he continues on with us. And my dear, sweet daughter Áine, Rós na Gaeilge, she is the living beat of my heart.

Introduction

I am so excited to be able to bring you *Heaven Help Us, Now!*, the single most comprehensive self-help guide to St. Jude Thaddeus the Apostle yet published. It is the first public fruit of my years of involvement with a saint who has rightfully captured the heartfelt devotion of so many people of so many backgrounds throughout the years. I started writing it as a personal thanksgiving to heaven for the incredible blessings my family and I have received through the intercession of St. Jude. I will just lay it out for you right now that my purpose is to inspire as many people as I can to pray to him for help with their most difficult situations. Calling on St. Jude in the manner I lay out in this book is a sure path to alleviating so much unnecessary suffering in the world.

The lessons in this book are perennial; however, the message seems particularly appropriate for these times! Just in the span of time I wrote this book we have had the COVID-19 pandemic, civil unrest and violence, crazy happenings in China, you name it – the list goes on. But whether the world is in chaos or at peace, in a way it really doesn't matter. I can't imagine that we will ever *not* need the help of heaven and the prayers of the Apostle Jude. After all, is there ever a time when there is nobody in need?

The man of the hour, St. Jude Thaddeus, is one of God's dearest friends. **He is the patron saint of *desperate difficulties, hopeless cases,*** *impossible situations,* **and** *lost causes.* People today do not follow saints the way they do entertainment celebrities. This is a shame; the saints are far more worthy of adulation. But Jude was the rare holy figure who rose to a mainstream celebrity status back in the 20ᵗʰ Century. It is about time for God's own "first responder" to make a comeback in the popular consciousness, given the distressing nature of our times.

I only want to ask you to do ONE THING: **give it a chance!** You have absolutely nothing to lose, and have a lot to potentially gain. Everything I lay out is solidly grounded in the truth – there is nothing made up or phony. **This is the real deal.** I encourage you to read on.

Heaven Help Us, Now! offers a fresh take on the devotion to St. Jude Thaddeus in my attempt to explain it to a new generation. There are many details included in other printed material on the saint which I do not include here. On the other hand, there is a lot here that I have not seen printed anywhere else. It's not the point of this book to put forth every known fact about the saint. In this I take inspiration from the Gospel of John as it stands in relation to the other three Gospels. St. John kind of does his own thing; he leaves out details about Jesus that are well covered in Matthew, Mark, and Luke, but has a large quantity of material unique only to his work and covered nowhere else.

The "fresh take" on St. Jude that I bring to the table is one of presentation; the substance is actually not new at all. I merely connect dots that are already there, rather than draw new dots. The faith expressed in these pages is the same faith Jude Thaddeus himself preached all those centuries ago, which he in turn received directly from Jesus Christ, the Son of God.

I have written this book with the goal of allowing it to be easily readable, edifying, and enjoyable to those who are not Catholic religious professionals, or even Catholic. The tone and style of this book are entirely my own. If you like or even love it, then great, I am honored. That's what I pray for, of course.

If you don't like it, I pray you will have pity on my attempt. As the writer of the Second Book of Maccabees said, "If it is well told and to the point, that is what I myself desired; if it is poorly done and mediocre, that was the best I could do" (15:38).

Editorial Notes

Some Comments on Usage and Terminology

You will notice that pronouns referring to God are capitalized, unless they are not capitalized in the source of a quote. Capitalizing "He" and "Him" is a pious tradition but not strictly necessary. However, I have found it to be a handy device for making the Lord stick out on the page, so I have made it standard in this book.

By **Gospel** we mean literally, "Good News." This is the final and definitive divine revelation given to us by Jesus Christ, the Son of God. By **Christian** we mean a baptized follower of Jesus Christ. As an adjective it refers to that which pertains to His teachings and to the community of His followers known as the **Church**. By **Catholic** we mean "total, universal," referring to the Church in which the *totality* of the Christian Gospel lives and which extends the Lord's *universal* invitation of salvation to all of mankind, regardless of background. This Church is headed by the bishop of Rome, the **Pope**, whom Jesus appointed to be the visible head of His Church. By **Orthodoxy** we mean correct belief, an adherence to absolute objective Truth as revealed in the Gospel and taught by the Church; the adjectival form of this word is **Orthodox**. I have capitalized this word and its variants, according to the usual Melkite Catholic practice.

The word "cult" properly means the reverential devotion or honor given to a saint; it comes from the Latin *cultus*. However, it has taken on a distinctly pejorative connotation in popular parlance. I made the judgement call to avoid the term in order to avert possible misunderstandings and to save the time and space that would be necessary to explain its proper meaning throughout the text (not everyone reads from beginning to end, a lot of readers skip around). Maybe I will expend such energy on promoting correct terminology some other time, but in this volume I want to get straight to the point – you and St. Jude Thaddeus.

The cult of St. Jude Thaddeus – that is, his *cultus* or devotion – is a practice of **popular piety**. His devotion is actually relatively popular in the conventional sense of being widely acclaimed and liked, but *popular* is used here in the sense of "relating to the people." *Piety* is the sense of reverence that prompts us to worship God.

Liturgy, on the other hand, is the official public worship of the Church. The prayers of the people draw their power from the liturgy, and in turn, lead people back to the liturgy (CCC 1675). And so, the St. Jude devotion should ideally bring people closer to the liturgical worship through which we access supernatural life.

Sources and References

This is a popular work, not an academic one, and as such I have tried to keep reference notes to a minimum. Their use is reserved for direct quotes of outside sources and certain obscure facts or claims. I have adopted a hybrid system for references, using in-text citations where I deemed it appropriate and endnotes otherwise.

On the other hand, you will find this book replete with references to scripture and the *Catechism of the Catholic Church*, and these citations are given in-text. The *Catechism* citations are simple enough, indicated by parentheses, inside of which are "CCC" followed by the *Catechism* paragraph number from which the cited information is drawn.

Scriptural citations are also in parentheses, inside of which are the abbreviation of the biblical book's title, the chapter, and the verse(s). So for instance, (Jn 21:24-24) means, "the Gospel of John, Chapter 21, verses 24 through 25."

In the case of the Psalms, most of them are numbered differently in the Hebrew and Greek versions from which modern translations are derived. I give the Hebrew numbering first, followed by the Greek in parentheses.

A list of abbreviations for cited books of the Bible is given below. The system used is that which is found in the *New American Bible*. As a side note, I get a bit of a chuckle that the abbreviation of Jude is "Jude."

All scriptural quotations are from the *Revised Standard Version, Second Catholic Edition* (RSV), unless otherwise noted.

Many sources were consulted for the research that underlies *Heaven Help Us, Now!*, but pride of place goes to the *Catechism of the Catholic Church*, and above all, to the Holy Bible.

Why these particular sources?

In the case of the *Catechism*, it was the fruit of a synod convoked by Pope St. John Paul II which proposed that a "compendium of all catholic doctrine regarding both faith and morals be composed."[1] The Pope proclaimed that the *Catechism,* "is a statement of the Church's faith and of catholic doctrine, attested to or illumined by Sacred Scripture, the Apostolic Tradition, and the Church's Magisterium. I declare it to be a sure norm for teaching the faith."[2] That is quite an endorsement from the top – and so, its pedagogical value is beyond compare.

As far as the Bible, what can I say? Quite simply, it is the very word of God. The Holy Church teaches that, "Sacred Scripture of both the Old and New Testament are like a mirror in which the pilgrim Church on earth looks at God."[3] The teaching of the Apostles, Jude Thaddeus among them, "is expressed in a special way in the sacred books." St. Paul tells us that, "all Scripture is inspired by God and profitable for teaching, for reproof, for correction, and for training in righteousness, that the man of God may be complete, equipped for every good work" (2 Tm 3:16). Thus, there is no way I was not going to mine the riches of divine revelation so I could set *Heaven Help Us, Now!* on the most solid possible foundation.

ABBREVIATIONS OF BOOKS OF THE BIBLE REFERENCED IN THIS VOLUME

Old Testament

Dt – Deuteronomy

Ex – Exodus

Gn – Genesis

Is – Isaiah

Jb – Job

1 Kgs – 1 Kings

2 Mc – 2 Maccabees

Prv – Proverbs

Ps – Psalms

Sir – Sirach

Wis – Wisdom

New Testament (Gospels in bold)

Acts – Acts of the Apostles

Col – Colossians

1 Cor – 1 Corinthians

Eph – Ephesians

Heb – Hebrews

Jas – James

Jn – **John**

Jude – Jude

Lk – **Luke**

Mk – **Mark**

Mt – **Matthew**

Phil – Philippians

1 Pt – 1 Peter

Rom – Romans

Rv – Revelation

1 Thes – 1 Thessalonians

2 Tm – 2 Timothy

TABLE OF CONTENTS

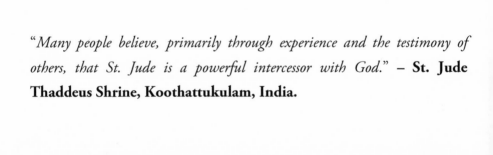

"*Many people believe, primarily through experience and the testimony of others, that St. Jude is a powerful intercessor with God.*" – **St. Jude Thaddeus Shrine, Koothattukulam, India.**

1

First Responder

"When I pray to St. Jude, I once more feel that there is hope and to despair would gain me nothing." – **Letter to *St. Jude's Journal*, August-September, 1961; reprinted on cover jacket of *Thank You, St. Jude* by Robert A. Orsi**

"I think about where I was a few months ago and how hopeless I felt, and now I have an amazing living situation, and an amazing job. Thank you so much St. Jude. You are always listening, you are always so generous with blessings and I am so so so thankful for everything you have given me. Thank you for not giving up on me and for giving me so many opportunities and miracles. I love you." – **Linda (website of the Franciscan Friars of the Atonement at Graymoor)**

Have you ever been in a desperate difficulty, or thought your case or that of a loved one was hopeless? Have you ever been stuck in an impossible situation, or fought for a lost cause?

I certainly have, many times over. In some cases, the result was personal tragedy. In other cases, I came out unscathed and stronger than ever.

Disaster is certainly easy enough to make happen, or to allow to happen. What is much harder to achieve is a positive outcome in a situation where you just don't have any control over the variables. Such situations drive many people absolutely nuts.

I am going to share with you my **secret weapon**, the reason I did not succumb to disaster once I started using it but rather came out on top of whatever challenge I faced. Many thousands of others also know this secret and use it to achieve the most astounding outcomes. The secret weapon is this: **devotion to St. Jude Thaddeus the Apostle**.

I'll tell you right now, in a nutshell, what this devotion is all about. You will be talking to a dead guy who lived about two thousand years ago and asking him to put in a good word with God on your behalf.

A faithful Catholic will recognize that this is just another way of describing *praying* to a saint. He knows that the saints are not truly dead but alive in heaven with God. He also knows that in no case do we ever give a saint the honor, worship, and adoration due to God alone – "praying" to them is just an honorific way of saying "talking" to them.

At the other end of the spectrum, there are people who will think that all of this is preposterous. But if you are in a jam, why would you be so dead set against praying in a manner that is proven to work? You truly have nothing to lose except the chance to have your situation solved! As the famous expression goes, "There are no atheists in foxholes."

Then there are others who are kind of in the middle. These are people who believe Christianity but are lax about prayer as a regular thing in their lives. Well, it's ironic, but sometimes a crisis is just what we need – a good kick in the pants that motivates us to get our priorities straight.

The very thing that makes a crisis a crisis – the real risk of tragic disaster – is a thing that happens all too often, unnecessarily. While everyone suffers in this life, and every single one of us must "take up his cross"

(Mk 8:34), we also have it in *our* power to save ourselves and others from situations outside our control.

Wait a minute, how does that make sense? We have it in our power to affect things that are outside of our power?

This oxymoronic proposition is a contradiction in appearance only. Here's how it actually works: we may not have direct power over a given situation, but we can appeal to God and gain access to *His* infinite power in order to achieve a desired result. And the operative factor in successfully affecting outcomes is the level to which we have the supernatural virtue of **faith**.

Ya Gotta Believe

One day after weekday Liturgy at Nativity of Our Lord Church I was talking to the parish priest, Fr. Iaroslav, and a fellow parishioner named Mark. I'll tell you the date – it was Columbus Day of 2020, October 12. I was nearly complete with the manuscript of *Heaven Help Us, Now!* and was quite excited telling the guys about it.

Mark spoke up. "You know, I prayed a novena to St. Jude when my son was born."

A novena is a prayer devotion recited on nine consecutive days, a very ancient Christian tradition.

"He was premature and had respiratory distress, tubes and wires all over his body. He was like that for eight days, and I prayed to St. Jude every day. On the ninth day, he was discharged."

My jaw dropped. It's not that I thought it wasn't possible – quite the opposite. It lent further evidence to me of the veracity of this book's premise. Like, wow. Jude's personal influence is everywhere, hidden away in the personal narratives of countless faithful people around the world who turned to him in times of need.

This is *real*.

Tapping Into a Deeper Reality

The supernatural realm is one of the domains of existence that is most ignored by mainstream culture. I am speaking of supernatural reality as understood by Christianity, not the distorted fictional depictions of the supernatural as put forward by the likes of Hollywood.

Indeed, dismissive attitudes about reality beyond our temporal existence are particularly common in the so-called developed world. In a way this is understandable because the supernatural, by its very nature, is not perceivable by the senses; talking about it in a serious manner requires at least a minimal belief in the possibility of its existence.

Even if this is understandable, it is a great shame. Most of the attention of mainstream popular culture is pointed in frivolous directions. Just do an internet search on "most popular celebrities," "trending celebrities," or something like that, and see what you get. Look around at the magazine covers in supermarkets. Check out the latest social media fads, particularly among young people.

Saints are rarely seen in mainstream culture in the early 21st century, at least in my experience. Perhaps one day they will be. And they should be, because saints are regular people who attained victory over the world, the flesh, and the devil. As such, they should be held up as figures of admiration and emulation. In addition, they help us on earth with their special ability to appeal directly to God because they are actually with God, face-to-face.

There was one bright, shining exception to the mainstream trend in recent times. That exception was St. Jude Thaddeus. Devotion to him took off in the United States at the end of the Roaring Twenties of the 20th century and continued with great intensity through the Great Depression, World War II, and the postwar era. From America, devotion to him radiated throughout the world. He was a household name even among non-Catholics. For instance, even today most people in the United States have probably heard of St. Jude Children's Research Hospital. But, alas, he is not nearly as well known in the early 21st century as he should be, and he should be since so many people stand to benefit from his assistance.

I believe it is time for a St. Jude revival.

Just In Time...

The introduction to the biblical Letter of Jude in the *New American Bible* says that it is, "an urgent note by an author who intended to write more fully." The particular crisis circumstances that St. Jude encountered spurred him to write his epistle to warn Christians who were in grave spiritual danger. Perhaps this is one reason God chose him to be the patron saint of hopeless causes.

I have written *Heaven Help Us, Now!* in a similar spirit, with a similar sense of urgency. The message of St. Jude Thaddeus could not be more timely. I had had an interest in this saint for much of my life and already knew a decent amount about him. But I first undertook serious research about Jude with a view to writing a book in November of 2019. Even then, I saw it as a timely matter of the utmost importance.

I started writing this as a much belated thanksgiving to the great saint for all the blessings my family and I received through his intercession. I held it as a sacred duty to share what I knew with others. It was just not right to keep this knowledge to myself when there were so many suffering souls out there who could benefit from the prayers of God's own "first responder."

2020

But then, 2020 hit. Oh, what a year. Even though I have more to write on Jude Thaddeus, and even though no one can possibly know what the future will hold, and even though the overwhelming majority of people reading *Heaven Help Us, Now!* will be doing so long after 2020 has passed, this book needed to come out in the aftermath of such an historic year when so many of us suffered so much.

The world was hit with the COVID-19 pandemic, infecting millions. And then, the associated economic shutdowns occurred, businesses closed, and livelihoods were destroyed. Communist China made moves for power, and America was beset by social unrest, violent riots, and skyrocketing violent crime in her cities.

Chicago in particular was hit with murder sprees reminiscent of wartime Baghdad and Kandahar. This is significant, because Chicago is St. Jude's special city; he is the patron saint of the Chicago Police Department. Dear Lord, he would help those brave law enforcement officers if they called upon him!

And he can help each and every one of us too, in the most amazing ways.

I am coming to you as **someone who was in the thick of it**. In fact, I wrote the great majority of this book in my spare time while serving as a National Guard soldier on New York's COVID-19 mission. Now, I would like to invite every single soul I can reach to join me in turning to this free source of supernatural assistance. Let's pray together, and we will work wonders!

Nothing to Lose, A Lot to Gain

It is crucial to keep in mind that St. Jude is not just some psychological construct that some people grasp onto for comfort, to make themselves feel better when life is going poorly. He is a *real* man (in every sense of the term), who lived on earth two millennia ago and who now lives forever with God in eternal bliss. Jesus granted him the special power to rescue us in desperate difficulties, hopeless cases, impossible situations, and lost causes.

If you believe already, then great, you know what I'm talking about. But if you don't believe, or you're skeptical, here's what I say: **Give it a chance – you have nothing to lose!** It doesn't cost you a penny. I'm pretty sure you have at least some interest since you are at least reading this sentence right now. So let's make a deal.

At least for the duration of this book, I'm asking you to suspend your disbelief and allow for the possibility that maybe, just *maybe*, there is something to this. There have been hundreds of thousands or even millions throughout the years who have sworn that St. Jude helped them. They just might have been onto something that taps into a deeper reality.

One of the best things we can do as a society is to revive the devotional culture which was such a distinct marker of Catholic Christianity for centuries, right up to the mid-late 20th century. We must do this in the same manner that one goes about reading the Bible – we must do it in the light of the Gospel as authoritatively taught by the One, Holy, Catholic, Apostolic Church.

The devotional culture never went away, but there is no doubt that it waned, along with religion generally, over a period of decades. The results are telling in the U.S., Ireland, Scotland, and other Western countries. We see an increase in apathy, atheism, an attraction to the false gospel of Marx; and there is a corresponding increase in immorality, violence, and an overall disrespect for the dignity of the human person. I am not making any claim that the world was all that saintly in past generations; however, I am saying that certain key elements of the human condition are trending in the wrong direction as the third millennium gets underway.

In fact, I'd say the Temple of God's Holy Spirit (i.e. the human body) is being desecrated in a more extreme, malicious, and widespread manner in society at large than was the case with the moneychangers in the Jerusalem Temple. The moneychangers infuriated the Lord Jesus so much that it was the only recorded instance in which He used physical force to chastise sinners during His earthly ministry (Jn 2:13-16). I shudder to think of Christ's judgement on today's evils on that big day when it's too late to say sorry.

The big point is that there are severe ills in society which lead to so much unnecessary suffering. There would be problems even in an ideal earthly society. This is because of our species' fallen nature. Ain't never gonna be such a thing as Utopia in this life!

Yet, we can mitigate much of the suffering by living a life of lively faith. Jesus teaches us that, "all things are possible to him who believes" (Mk 9:23). So, it would be wise to put our faith in Christ, which is the main thing, and to take full advantage of His bonus gift to us – the friendship and help of St. Jude Thaddeus.

Jude is the saint of the extremities, who reaches out to the vulnerable and the outcasts, to those on the fringes of popular consciousness. We are not on the outside to him, we are central!

To get a better idea of Jude's reach, we can learn a lot from India. This country was one of the first to receive the Gospel and one in which the influence of Jude Thaddeus was strong. The particular liturgy the Christian Indians used for the Mass almost from the time of Christ was reputed to have been written by Jude Thaddeus himself. His legacy is ancient and his memory has been honored for millennia.

And yet, there has also been a strong recent revival of devotion to him. The St. Jude Shrine of Koothattukulam in the southern Indian region of Malabar was only founded in the year 2000. St. Jude covers the extremities of time – ancient and modern. He also covers the extremities of geography, shining his light in places considered peripheral to world elites but central to the human souls who inhabit those regions.

The website of the Koothattukulam shrine sums up the devotion pretty well: "We pray to St. Jude as a brother, pleading with him to join in our prayer before the Most High... It is God, however, who answers our prayers and grants us all good gifts. St. Jude will usher those who call on him, to a safe path from sufferings," and these sufferings are listed as:

- ailments beyond human limits
- incurable diseases which exceed the reach of medical sciences
- poverty
- depression
- overwhelming stress
- distress in family
- devilry

The stories of St. Jude's intercession are so numerous that they could never be condensed into a single volume. What I will do here is give you a representative sample of real-life vignettes, taken from a randomized variety of trustworthy sources.

Funny enough, when I got to writing this part of the chapter I received a letter in the mail from my Aunt Kathleen, out of the blue. She knew I had a devotion to St. Jude Thaddeus. Well, what she sent me was a promotional newsletter of the St. Jude Shrine of the Pallottine Fathers in Baltimore, the oldest in the U.S.

It had within it some of the testimonials that are common in such publications. I was like, "Ah, what perfect and serendipitous timing! I shall include these."

And, so I have.

Here are the sources, followed by the testimonial vignettes:

1. Pallottine newsletter from Aunt Kathy.
2. Website of the Franciscan Friars of the Atonement at Graymoor (atonementfriars.org/st-jude-prayer-circle).
3. *Saint Anthony and Saint Jude* by Mitch Finley.
4. *Thank You, St. Jude* by Robert A. Orsi.
5. *The Saint of the Impossible* by Brian Morgan.

MEDICAL CRISIS

"I was recently diagnosed with breast cancer. The tumor is very large. When I found out, I immediately started a Novena to St. Jude asking for his intercession. I prayed that the cancer would be contained and not spread throughout my body. I started undergoing many tests to determine the status of the cancer and the method of treatment. Today, I was called (three days after my Novena ended) by my doctor and told that the cancer is contained and has not spread. Thank you St. Jude for the gift of life. I will be starting another Novena for the success of the treatment." – **Pat (Pallottine newsletter)**

"Thank You to St. Jude: Thank you St. Jude for your powerful intercession and healing our family specially our Mom from COVID-19." – **Norman (website of the Franciscan Friars of the Atonement at Graymoor)**

EMPLOYMENT & CAREER

"St. Jude helped me after more than a year of despair and frustration seeking employment. After praying to St. Jude for only 5 days, I was employed in a dream job in a position that will surely define the rest of my career. I owe it all to St. Jude and God's grace. Thank you St. Jude!" – **Anonymous (Pallottine newsletter)**

FINANCIAL RELIEF & SUCCESS

"Thank you God's special Saint, Saint Jude Thaddeus for answering my desperate prayers for financial help; our large medical bill has been dismissed! Clients and income are streaming my way with faith in St. Jude and as my financial desperation prayers are being answered. Thank you Jesus, I trust in you!" – **Jeanine Delaney (Graymoor website)**

LEGAL ISSUES

"Maria F. … has a cousin who is an assistant district attorney in Arizona. He asked Maria to pray for a special favor, so Maria began a novena to Saint Jude for her cousin.

'About seven days later,' Maria said, 'he called to tell me his prayer had been answered. The Supreme Court was hearing an appeal [regarding] a state law. If it ruled against the district attorney's office, he would have been personally liable. … He could have been a defendant in over three hundred [lawsuits] by people he had prosecuted. It looked very bad, [but] the next day – about seven days into the novena – the judge ruled for the state. My cousin called immediately to tell me.'" – **(Finley, p. 124)**

ADDICTION

"My husband started drinking a good deal and spent many nights away from home. Needless to say, my four children and I were lonely. After many prayers to St. Jude and Our Blessed Mother my husband is home every night and is not drinking. We are a happy family and I know it was made possible through the intercession of St. Jude." – **(Orsi, p. 192)**

GENERAL EMOTIONAL DISTRESS

"Thank you St. Jude for keeping me from being depressed on a regular basis. You listened to me. Thank you." – **Dolores (Graymoor website)**

COURTING, DATING, LOOKING TO MEET SOMEONE SPECIAL

Brian Morgan tells of a Mumbai woman who taught her children to pray to St. Jude. "One of her daughters threatened to hang St Jude upside down outside her window if she didn't find a beau. Jude apparently enjoys a joke, because the loveless lass ended up with a stream of suitors." – **(Morgan, pp. 131-33)**

GETTING PREGNANT

"Anthony and Natalina D'Souza, from Goa, in the south of India, were childless for seven years. Nattie tried various therapies to become pregnant and consulted specialists, but her case, she was told, was hopeless. A friend, Motti Mama (meaning, so I'm told, Fat Aunt), gave Nattie a novena to St Jude. The desperate woman made the novena. She conceived and named her baby girl Judith, after Jude." – **(Morgan, p. 131)**

SAFE CHILDBIRTH

"In 1947, Jane G. of Springfield, Illinois, was pregnant with her and her husband's third child. The due date had passed, and the doctor determined that the baby was in a breech position. 'Sister Mary Aquinas, a Franciscan friend, suggested we make a novena to Saint Jude,' Jane said. 'We did, and on October 28, Saint Jude's feast day, the baby turned himself to the proper position and was born within a few hours.'" – **(Finley, p. 91)**

FAMILY PEACE

"Thank you for answering my prayers regarding my Great Aunt and Uncle as to allow them to make amends and come together to celebrate the Christmas holiday." – **Dustin (Graymoor website)**

ANIMALS

"St. Jude

Thank you for answering my prayers about the health of our kitten. I am forever grateful for your intercessions." – **Jennifer T. (Graymoor website)**

ACADEMIC SUCCESS

"My dear St. Jude, with all my heart, THANK YOU SO MUCH FOR GETTING ME THROUGH MY NURSING CLINICAL ROTATION SUCCESSFULLY!!! My 9-day novena prayers were answered miraculously as always!!! I will continue to make your name known the best way I can!!! I will be your faithful client forever!!!!" – **M.G. (Graymoor website)**

MISC.
"Dear St Jude –

Thank you for your guidance to help me succeed on stage last night. I am so grateful at how things went – you provide me with so much support and comfort to help assuage any concerns or fears I have. I am truly thankful to you and to God for this. Thank you." – **Del (Graymoor website)**

I Believe in Truth *and* Facts

Heaven Help Us, Now! is about you, not me. But just so that you know that I know what I'm talking about, I will share with you a small bit of my story.

I came to my knowledge of how prayer works through a whole lot of research, trial, and error ... and success. My foundational presuppositions are based on the divine revelation taught by Catholic Christianity. But we are not going to get too technical here; suffice it to say that I come from a point of view that is based on the Truth. And I have good reason to believe that this Truth I believe is actually *the* Truth, the whole Truth, and nothing but the Truth.

No matter how strong, how smart, how talented a person might be they are actually pretty weak. We all are. Think of how easy it is for people to be hurt or killed, how our lifetimes are a brief microsecond in the big scheme of things, how we are so tiny in comparison to the earth that the scale is similar to bacteria on a pebble. Never mind that we hardly control anything – not when we're born, not today's weather, not the number of hydrogen and oxygen atoms required for a water molecule.

Don't get me wrong, I was, am, and always will be the primary active agent in my life, God willing. There is no passivity in me, no way. I have accomplished a lot in my life through my own efforts. However, even my own efforts, my capacity to *do* things, is a free gift from God for which I need to be grateful. Jesus is the vine, we are His branches, and without Him we can do nothing (Jn 15:5).

And that is the point. If we are dependent on Him even for what we do of our own volition, how much more are we dependent on him for what we don't control!

And this is where God's first responder comes in. The Lord gave us St. Jude Thaddeus to help us cover that X-factor in life, that trepidatious unknown territory beyond our control.

St. Jude Saved My Family

Perhaps some day I will share more of my story, or at least the particulars that demonstrate to me unmistakable evidence of heaven's direct intervention. The broad outlines will suffice here.

St. Jude Thaddeus saved my family.

A few years back, my wife Deirdre and I had already been married a few years and had already suffered the pain of miscarriage. And then, my wife was hit unexpectedly with a medical issue which put her ability to have children in jeopardy.

If it was God's will for us to be a childless couple, then so be it. His will be done, not ours. But I turned to His friend St. Jude to please ask the Master to have pity on us, to allow Deirdre to get through this. Not only did she come out of the situation unscathed, but we conceived within a month after, right around Jude's October 28 feast day.

And that baby turned out to be my beautiful daughter Áine.

My gratitude knows no bounds. This is why I undertook writing *Heaven Help Us, Now!* St. Jude's ability to help people in extreme need extends to all who call upon him. But to call on him, you have to know about him! And more than that, you really cannot go into it blindly, yelling, "Hey Jude," and then giving up in frustration if things don't happen to your immediate gratification. Nor can you approach him in a cocky, testing manner or expect him to perform some magic trick. That's not how any of this works.

Fear not! In the pages of this book you will find out what does work. Gratitude was my motivational catalyst for writing *Heaven Help Us, Now!*, and my main purpose has been to explain the devotion to St. Jude Thaddeus to as many people as I could reach. By doing so, I hope to honor this great saint and to share the mercy, peace, and love of Christ as far and wide as possible.

I prayed to St. Jude every single day while writing this book; I prayed that he would assist me in writing it. I thank him for his guidance in scrawling whatever is good in these pages. But of course, any imperfections are my own and I take full responsibility for them. Yet I do want to say that since he has answered me in everything else I have ever asked of him, I have no reason to think that he has backed out of assisting me now.

So God bless, and enjoy the rest!

2

Who

The big "who" question is this: **Who** benefits from devotion to St. Jude Thaddeus?

The answer: **You** do. And **I** do. **We** *all* do. Actually, **anyone** can call upon him for help. You do not have to be a member of the Catholic Church. You do not even have to have any professed religion. All you have to have is an open mind and just enough nascent faith to give it a chance, to concede the *possibility* that all this stuff is real.

I will be upfront: it is ultimately all about Jesus, whose name means "the Lord saves." But we are not getting into doctrinal issues or any such intellectually profound matters here. There is certainly a time and place for that. Right now, we are just concerned with getting you or someone you know out of a difficult circumstance.

Rescuing individuals from immediate and present suffering is St. Jude's specialty. These are the situations in which the saving power of the Gospel is most tangible. One may be a faithful Christian who fully believes everything the Church teaches. But much of the faith is conceptually abstract, and it is difficult to concentrate on abstractions when you are about to lose your home, or just got diagnosed with a debilitating illness, or cannot figure out how to finish the semester without failing your courses.

The joy experienced by believers who know that they received relief and solutions from heaven gives the Gospel a sensory reality that abstract belief cannot provide. For those who are already true believers, such signs and wonders serve to confirm the faith they already have. For those on shakier ground, heavenly intervention that can be perceived by the senses can open one's eyes and heart to exploring the Gospel further.

Babies are fed with milk before they move onto solid food; the Gospel works in the same manner (1 Cor 3:1-2; Heb 5:11-14). Infants need to feel safe and provided for – this goes just as much for infants in Christ as for infants in the body. Heck, even mature people need to feel secure and loved. St. Jude Thaddeus is for people at every level of faith.

In order to call on him for help, it's fine if you are a sinner and it's even better if you know you are one (Lk 18:9-14). I'll tell you right now, I am a sinner and I know I am. I do my best not to sin but I succumb to my fallen nature far more often than I am comfortable with. But while I do fear the Lord because this is the only wise attitude to have (Prv 9:10), I do not live my life in anxiety (Mt 6:25-34). I take comfort from the words of Jesus: "Those who are well have no need of a physician, but those who are sick; I came not to call the righteous, but sinners" (Mk 2:17).

He came to save us – He came to save *us*!

And His sacrificial death on the Cross is the means by which He accomplished our salvation. His Father will not let His death be in vain and extends His mercy to all of us who turn to Him with sorrow for our sins.

The ability of St. Jude to help us get out of trouble is an extension of God's own power. The Lord delights in working through His creatures. Of course, we can appeal to God directly and should do so. This is why Jesus gave us the Lord's Prayer (the Our Father). But to give proper glory to God, we must invoke His holy ones as well. First and foremost among these is Mary – the eternal Virgin, the Theotokos, the Mother of God. We should be invoking her frequently.

After God and the Blessed Mother, we have the angels and saints. They all have a particular role to play, and centuries of pious tradition make clear that Jude Thaddeus was assigned by God with the special role of bringing "visible and speedy help where help is almost despaired of," as the prayer says (see Chapter 8, Prayer 4). Aren't we lucky!

A Brief Tour of the Universe

I just want to make sure we are on the same page about how everything works, so I will go over some of the bare-bone basics here. Nothing being laid out below is new information; I'm just summarizing some key points of what is already known.

At some point way back, the universe began – matter, energy, and time itself came into being. "Before" this there was nothing except being itself. This ultimate reality, the one whose self-description is, "I am who am" (Ex 3:14) is the being we know as "God." This God is omnipotent (all powerful), omniscient (all knowing), and omnibenevolent (all good; infinite love). He has no beginning and no end, is eternal in every way, and does not change. He *is* perfection. He brought everything that is not Him into existence *ex nihilo*, as the Latin goes, "out of nothing."

We can figure some things out about the physical universe through systematic empirical investigation, that is, through the intellectual venture we call "science." We know much less about the preternatural world. However, it is certain that God created spiritual beings who exist entirely beyond this universe. Some are good and holy and live in the presence of God. "Angel" is their umbrella designation. There are also fallen angels who are the same as good angels in substance but who are evil. These are known as "devils" or "demons," and the chief one among them is known as *the* devil, or Satan. Although these beings subsist outside the natural universe, their influence on human affairs is profound.

The study of how galaxies, stars, and planets were formed is quite fascinating but not our concern here. They are not alive, but we are. At a certain point, on this earth (and possibly on other planets) God brought biological life into being.

Since we can actually study earthly life forms with our senses and our intellect, it is apparent that all of it is stunning in its diversity, complexity, and beauty. The thing that is really unique about our own species is that we have a dual existence. We are part of both the natural and supernatural orders – we have both a natural body and a supernatural soul (CCC 327). Humans are at the top of the hierarchy of creation in the natural universe because we are the only physical creatures with a spiritual soul made in the image and likeness of God (Gn 1:27).

When we say "*creat*ure," we're not just talking about little critters running around; we mean anything *creat*ed, that is, anything that is not God. We humans might create things in a secondary manner, but God alone brings things into existence out of nothing – He alone is *the* Creator.

The original condition of the human race was one of innocence and goodness. The Church teaches that, "the first man was not only created good, but was also established in friendship with his Creator and in harmony with himself and with the creation around him" (CCC 374). Such was the wonderful state of existence of Adam and his wife Eve, our first parents. They lived in "original justice," which is defined as, "the inner harmony of the human person, the harmony between man and woman, and finally the harmony between the first couple and all creation" (CCC 376).

Surely, this was too good of a thing to mess up. But mess it up they did. They willingly chose to disobey God, even though it was easily within their power to obey. Their disobedience was prompted by the devil tempting them, but the external influence did not override their free will in choosing evil. As such, they stood guilty before God.

They committed the original sin, and lost original justice for all of us. In effect, the "spiritual DNA" of humanity was altered. The resulting fall of man did not result in our premature extinction, however. God still loved us dearly and fully intended to save mankind.

The narrative of these primordial events is contained in the first few chapters of Genesis, the first book of the Bible.

And so, the Lord allowed our ancestors to wander about, filling the earth and subduing it. Humans settled in every continent except Antarctica, and societies developed diverse and unique cultures suited to their individual environments.

Agriculture was discovered, animals were domesticated, and writing was invented. Civilizations appeared at certain times and places. When mankind had reached a certain maturity, the Lord God revealed Himself in the Middle East to a man we call Abraham. The descendants of Abraham's grandson Jacob, who was also known as Israel, were the nation that God chose for Himself. The nation itself was named Israel, and the people are also known as Jews, after Jacob's son Judah (Yehudah, Judas, Jude – all versions of the same name).

At a certain point, when mankind in general and the Jewish people in particular had developed to such a state that God knew it was time to make His definitive revelation, He sent us Jesus Christ. The name Jesus means "the Lord saves," as we mentioned, and Christ means "Messiah" or "anointed one." This man, Jesus Christ, is the eternal Word of God, His only Son.

"In the beginning was the Word, and the Word was with God, and the Word was God" (Jn 1:1). He is both God and man, the king of all that exists. He chose a group of twelve men to be His closest followers and to disseminate the Good News, the Gospel, that He was entrusting to them. One of these men was His kinsman Jude Thaddeus.

The teaching of Christ was one thing – that was to be transmitted intact across the generations because it was and is safeguarded by His Holy Spirit. The real work of His earthly ministry was not His preaching *per se*, but His Passion, Death, and Resurrection. The whole reason that God became man (while remaining God) was so that He could be slaughtered like an animal. He allowed Himself to reach full maturity, and then to be falsely accused, sentenced to death, and brutally tortured then executed.

He did this all for us. This was the price that had to be paid for the gates of heaven to open to humanity, the gates that were shut upon the expulsion of Adam and Eve from the original earthly perfection of Eden. This does not mean everyone goes to heaven, but it does mean that it is now possible to go to heaven.

By the way, Jesus got the last laugh, as God always does. Christ spent His period of bodily death with the souls of the just who had died before His coming, and He brought these souls the Good News. On the third day after His execution on the Cross, His body came back to life. The body and soul of our Lord were reunited, heaven's gate was unlocked, and a new era of glory in the history of the universe began.

So, where does the end of the human story leave us? There are two possibilities for each individual one of us.

The Happy End

Christ is alive forever, not just as the eternal God but as a physical man, never to die again. And we humans now know heaven exists and that we are invited to eternal Paradise. We take up His invitation to eternal life by becoming a part of Him, by joining His body – also known as the One, Holy, Catholic, Apostolic Church. It is that communion of the faithful which is visibly headed on Earth by the successor of St. Peter the "Rock," the bishop who is known in eastern parlance as the Pope of Rome.

Some of the best writings on the nature of what the Church is in its essence are found in the Bible, in the letters of St. Paul:

"Now you are the body of Christ and individually members of it" (1 Cor 12:27).

"He [*Jesus Christ*] is the head of the body, the Church" (Col 1:18).

The consummation of human history is *marital* in both symbology and substance. "Husbands, love your wives, as Christ loved the Church and gave himself up for her … husbands should love their wives as their own bodies. He who loves his wife loves himself … as Christ does the Church, because we are members of his body" (Eph 5:25, 28-30). Paul then digs down deeper to the roots of this profundity. He refers back to the primordial origin of human marriage itself as described in Genesis, the first book of the Bible. "'For this reason a man shall leave his father and mother and be joined to his wife, and the two shall become one flesh.' This is a great mystery, and I mean in reference to Christ and the Church" (Eph 5:31-32).

By the way, this is why we are not married to other people in heaven. If we are so fortunate as to make it there, we are married to God the Son! He Himself tells us that, "in the resurrection they neither marry nor are given in marriage, but are like the angels in heaven" … "for I tell you that in heaven their angels always behold the face of my Father who is in heaven" (Mt 22:30; 18:10). Seeing the face of God is the fulfillment of every drive and desire that humans were created to have; this is what is called the "Beatific Vision."

It is **the absolute perfection of infinite mercy, peace, and love**.

Call me crazy, but I'd say there is no doubt that this is the preferred destiny of mankind.

The Bad End

The only other destiny, and the one I hope nobody prefers, is to **go to hell**. A soul that is condemned will be in humiliation before Christ our Lord who will pronounce the judgement: "Depart from me, you cursed, into the eternal fire prepared for the devil and his angels" (Mt 25:41). And then that's that.

Torture, pain, and sorrow without relief or end.

This is frankly the most terrifying thing I can imagine; I beg the Lord's mercy for all our souls. I am not saying this part to be scary, it's just that Jesus told us about the existence of hell. He, the Word of God Himself, *revealed* it to us. Thus, I think it would only be wise to take His words at face value.

This Is the End...

Once the status of our soul is sealed by the death of our body, it is permanent and irrevocable for all eternity. There is only saved or damned.

By the way, I do want to briefly mention **Purgatory** in order to clear up any confusion. It is something like hell because it is a "place" of suffering, but it is "temporary" in duration. It is a tremendous mercy that the Lord has extended to us, to allow us to get our imperfections fixed and to pay off our debt before going to live with Him. The relevant paragraphs of the *Catechism* are 1030-1032. I'll quote the first of these in full here:

All who die in God's grace and friendship, but still imperfectly purified, are indeed assured of their eternal salvation; but after death they undergo purification, so as to achieve the holiness necessary to enter the joy of heaven. (CCC 1030).

Knowing all of this about heaven and hell is a profound motivator to get it right in this life and to help others to do the same. Mercifully, we get innumerable "second" chances in this life. But fair warning, we get absolutely no chance after we die – Purgatory only applies to those who are already saved at the time they pass from this life, "who die in God's grace and friendship." There are no post-mortem conversions.

The really crazy thing is that humans didn't know any of this with clarity until the Son of God gave us His definitive deposit of faith when He walked among us. Even what had already been revealed in the Old Testament was now understood in its fullness through the light of the Gospel. His revelation was and is truly revolutionary.

This Gospel is a perpetual source of comfort for our souls. Now, finally, we as a species know the reason for our existence and what happens to us when we die – Good News indeed!

I think it's interesting to note that it wasn't all that long ago that Jesus redeemed the world. Two thousand years is only about 60 generations. In the big scheme of things, that's nothing.

We are truly blessed to be living in this era of light, the "end times." Since most people in the world at the time of this writing do not accept Christ, it is our sacred duty of neighborly charity to help correct this tragedy. The devotion to St. Jude Thaddeus helps us to do this.

One Big, Happy Family

It is important to note that devotion to this one saint, Jude Thaddeus the Apostle, does not in any way preclude loyalty or devotion to any other holy men, women, and angels in heaven. It is quite easy to choose your own crew of heavenly benefactors who will help you in this life and with whom you will be able to share a face-to-face friendship in the next.

We can demonstrate this with the example of St. Gerard Majella, the 18th century Italian who is famed as the patron of expectant mothers. He was first and foremost dedicated to God, then to the Mother of God. Then came the rest of heaven:

Besides the Twelve Apostles, he daily honored his Guardian Angel, St. Joseph, Sts. Joachim and Anne, St. John the Baptist, St. Bernard, St. Philip Neri, St. Mary Magdalene the Penitent, St. Francis Xavier, St. Teresa, St. Francis of Assisi, St. Felix Cantalice, the Forty Martyrs, the Saint of his birthday, and also the Saint of the day on which he is to die. But nothing equaled his tender devotion to the Archangel Michael.[4]

Incidentally, St. Michael plays a big part in the St. Jude story. The Apostle is the only biblical author to give Michael the title of "Archangel," the designation he is universally known by today. In recognition of this, the two medals I have flanking the Crucifix on my personal Rosary are of St. Jude and St. Michael.

The bigger point is that the Church is the communion of saints. We are all in this together. And you can choose your friends from among those who are in heaven right now, just like you can on Earth. It should be emphasized that just as devotion to St. Jude does not preclude devotion to any other saint, choosing particular saints you are attracted to is in no way dishonoring any of the other holy ones.

For instance, when St. Jude Thaddeus first came to major public prominence in America in 1929, there were two major statues in Our Lady of Guadalupe Church in Chicago. One was of St. Thérèse of Lisieux, the other of St. Jude the Apostle. Initially, Thérèse was placed in the more prominent position. But the faithful inexplicably started gathering to pray in front of the statue of Jude, a fairly unfamiliar figure at the time.

Crowds for St. Jude grew with each passing week. In response to this surprising turn of popularity, the statues were switched – St. Jude was placed forward in the more prominent spot and St. Thérèse was put to the side.

Now, does this mean that Thérèse of Lisieux is any less of a saint? No way!

She is forever revered as the Little Flower and has a tremendous following. And even though she lived in recent times (d. 1897), her renown and spiritual insight is such that she was declared by St. John Paul II to be a Doctor of the Church, an exceptionally rare and special title.

It's just that divine providence set aside this time, place, and circumstance for Jude Thaddeus; other times, places, and circumstances are set aside by God for other saints. We are attracted to those who fit our individual uniqueness. And any which way you cut it, the communion of saints is one big happy family.

Who Is St. Jude Thaddeus?

So, who exactly is St. Jude Thaddeus? If we are going to call him for help, it's only fitting that we know something of his biographical details.

First and foremost, he was one of the twelve men called by Jesus Christ to be one of His Apostles. He is known by a few different names in the Bible. In the Gospel of Luke (6:16) and the Acts of the Apostles (1:13) he is called "Jude of James" (this is the literal translation, non-RSV). In the Epistle of Jude (v. 1), which he wrote, he calls himself "Jude brother of James." The Gospel of John (14:22) has him as "Judas, not the Iscariot." The Gospels of Mark (3:18) and Matthew (10:3) list him as "Thaddeus."

He was also a kinsman of the Messiah. He is listed in the Gospels as a "brother" of Jesus, that is, a close male relative of roughly the same generation.

His second name distinguishes him from others with the name Judas – especially Judas Iscariot. The meaning of "Thaddeus" also expresses the qualities of his character – *hearty, amiable, loving, magnanimous*. Two other forms of Thaddeus you may come across are Lebbaeus (found in some manuscripts of Matthew's Gospel) and Addai (a later Aramaic/Syriac form).

The single most famous deed for which Jude Thaddeus is known is the conversion of Abgar, king of Edessa. The Apostle had cured this king of a hopeless case of leprosy with a miraculously imprinted image of Christ, most likely the burial shroud of the Lord. The episode has implications far beyond being an entertaining story from the early days of the Church. His curing of a king given up for dead with a visible relic and the subsequent conversion of a pagan city is the original basis for:

1. Jude Thaddeus being honored as the patron of hopeless cases and the impossible.

2. The sacred Christian tradition of giving honor to holy images and objects.

Unknown and Forgotten

There was a time when he was known as "the forgotten saint" or "the unknown saint." This would be an ironic appellation for him nowadays, since Jude Thaddeus is probably one of the best known saints in the world. But there was a time when he was relatively obscure in western Europe and America. Ironically, this probably helped him to develop a following as the patron of lost causes. The fact that he was so forgotten and unknown led to a connection between Jude and the forgotten, unknown members of society.

There was some precedent for veneration of Jude Thaddeus in the Christian West before modern times. St. Bernard of Clairvaux was buried with a relic of Jude (12th century), and Christ Himself spoke to St. Birgitta of Sweden about the amiable Thaddeus in a vision (14th century).

Rises In The East...

But the Apostle has always been a major saint in parts of the Christian East since the very beginning. Armenia was the first nation in the world to adopt Christianity as its official religion back in 301. St. Thaddeus is honored along with St. Bartholomew as one of the founders of the Church in the country, and so holds a position with the Armenians roughly analogous to that of St. Patrick with the Irish.

In addition, as pointed out above, the oldest Eucharistic liturgy in the Catholic Church is attributed to Thaddeus and his disciple Mari. That is to say, their names are attached to it. Even if they did not compose the exact wording that has come down to us, they are responsible for the primitive nucleus of the liturgy.

This is an aspect of the St. Jude devotion that has not been much explored previously; it deserves further research because the implications are truly mind-blowing. It means that our favorite saint was intimately involved in every Mass that was said from Mesopotamia to China for the first millennium and a half of Christianity. Praise to Jesus, the *Anaphora of Addai and Mari* is still used by the Chaldean Catholic Church (hearthland: Iraq) and the Syro-Malabar Catholic Church (hearthland: India).

... Sets In The West

The modern explosion of devotion to Jude Thaddeus was ignited in Chicago, Illinois, at the climax of the Roaring Twenties. I have already referred to the phenomenon earlier in this chapter. From Chicago, his fame spread like wildfire throughout the United States. It was as if the

Lord was preparing the people for the Great Depression, which struck shortly after St. Jude burst onto the American Catholic scene.

The Apostle gave comfort and relief to legions of suffering souls during the tough period of the 1930's, an era when hope was in short supply (if one were only to look at things from a secular perspective). Jude continued his mission throughout the Second World War, as millions of American servicemen fought and defeated tyranny.

The wonderful thing was that Jude's popularity did not abate in the post-war era of prosperity. If anything, his influence spread. In fact, Jude gained something of a celebrity saint status. The actor and comedian Danny Thomas and his founding of St. Jude Children's Research Hospital had some part in this.

But the bigger factor was a track record of successful and documented intercession on behalf of the faithful, an intercession that spanned back over decades and centuries. St. Jude's success in rescuing souls and bringing them to Christ bred even greater success in the wider Apostolic endeavor of preaching the Gospel, a success that continues to this day.

3

What

Now we get to the real meat of what the devotion to St. Jude Thaddeus involves. At its heart, it is simply *prayer*. However, like most words in any language, many people who might have a passive understanding of what a word like "prayer" means would be hard pressed to give an accurate definition. That's okay, this one is simple.

Prayer is simply talking to heaven. It can be formal, public, and liturgical; it can be informal, private, and spontaneous; or it can be something in between. All of these different modes of prayer have their place. They all involve talking to real people who actually hear you.

One of the differences between traditional Christianity (usually called "Catholic" or "Orthodox") and more recent forms (usually under the umbrella label "Protestant") is the veneration of saints. I want to set the record straight here. Only God, God alone, is entitled to worship. This is basic First Commandment stuff.

The saints and angels are His friends. We do *not* worship or adore any of them. And in the case of the human saints (except for the Virgin Mary), they were just like all of us in that they had the "original sin" inherited from Adam on their souls.

We absolutely do not worship them; we can, however, speak to them. This conversation with holy men, women, and angels in heaven is known as "praying." It is the same word used when referring to *speaking to God*, the only being to whom we give adoration. And while we do not adore them, we do *venerate* the holy ones. This means that we give them reverential honor and respect. They are our seniors, who have led the way in getting to where we ourselves want to go.

Of all the billions of people who have ever lived (about 110 billion, according to one count)[5] only a few thousand have had their personal sanctity publicly recognized by the Church such that the title of "saint" is bestowed upon them. This is according to the will of God, whose Holy Spirit guides His Church in recognizing those whose life example points the way to heaven for us.

The Lord takes delight in His creatures. Each has its purpose, and the saints have the special purpose of interceding with God for us. They have been proven worthy of Jesus Christ by their trials on earth, in the valley of tears, and now they gaze directly upon God as He truly is for all eternity. They are in a position to put in a good word for us.

Of all the saints, the Virgin Mary has a special place – she is the greatest of anyone or anything that exists except for God. Her hymn during the Divine Liturgy rightfully praises her as "more honorable than the Cherubim, and beyond compare more glorious than the Seraphim, who, a virgin gave birth to God the Word, you truly the Theotokos [i.e. *God-bearer*] we magnify."

After the Mother of God, we have the rest of the saints. Because of their earthly lives of cooperating with the Holy Spirit, they have been rewarded in heaven with an individualized fullness of grace. That is, their heavenly reward is exactly tailored to their earthly holiness. The customized reward each saint receives has an impact on how they pray for us in the Lord's presence.

While all the saints pray for our salvation in a general sense, the Holy Spirit grants each one a discreet domain of patronage. This allows their intercession to be focused effectively, and in a manner consonant with the purpose God created them for. So, for example, Blaise is the patron saint of throats, Macdara is the patron of fishermen in the Conamara region of Ireland, and Jude Thaddeus… well, his duties are among the weightiest of any of the saints. He is truly God's own first responder.

The Right Stuff

So, how do we start? The first things we need are the correct attitudes and internal dispositions. Just like the hero astronauts in the early days of NASA, we need "the right stuff." Let's take a look at our shortlist below:

1. **Faith.** The more faith you have the better. But if you're just starting off and you don't have all that much faith, and you're suspicious of prayer actually working, that's okay. The very fact that you are willing to give it a shot indicates that you have *some* faith. So let's just start with what we got. It's inevitable that your faith will increase as you keep your heart open to experience the Lord's saving power through St. Jude's prayers.

2. **Personal Affection.** Belief without feeling is a dead, lifeless thing. Put your *heart* into it. Cleanse hatred from your soul and fill yourself with love and hope. The way to do this is to ask God for these virtues. Even

though St. Jude tends to be called on for tangible intentions, he will help you achieve virtue as well. Cultivating a virtuous and forgiving heart will, in turn, allow for a greater likelihood that your intention will be granted (see Mt 5:23-24 about reconciling with your brother before approaching God).

3. **Make a Promise.** People generally don't like ungrateful mooches. You don't even have to be religious to understand this. So, promise to do something for St. Jude and then do it. Chapter 9 is all about this. We are not strictly required to make a promise but people who turn to Jude generally do so anyways. Intuitively, it just feels right.

"Lord, Open My Lips" (Ps 51(50):17)

Next, we have the actual talking part. The specific prayers to St. Jude are contained in Chapter 8. They can and should be said in conjunction with prayers to God and the Theotokos, the basic ones of which can be found in Appendix B. See what combination of prayers is the best fit for you – what prayers capture your heart, which ones seem to work best, which ones you develop a personal affection for because of how they engage you on a spiritual level.

Start in your heart. Speak to him, "St. Jude, help me out." Then you can launch into the recitation of the prayers. These prayers are powerful because of the holy sentiments they express, and they have been made particularly holy through generations of use by the faithful devotees of St. Jude.

It is important to strike a balance in the life of prayer. Spontaneity in calling on Jude is welcome and encouraged. It bears witness to a lively faith. However, relying on such internal urgings without the structure of regular and formal prayer leaves you at the mercy of your emotions. The minimal discipline required to do a nine-day novena, let's say, structures our petitions to heaven in a manner that shows commitment and the use of our human, rational mind.

On the other hand, leaning too much on the formal words leads to an imbalance of another kind. Praying is **not** "magic." It is **not** composed of superstitious incantations. Jesus warns against this. Of course, He is the ultimate authority on *everything*; but as the *Word* of God He directs our attention in a special way to the use of language, words, and prayer. He says, "And in praying do not heap up empty phrases as the Gentiles do; for they think that they will be heard for their many words. Do not be like them" (Mt 6:7-8).

Scatterbrain

It is natural for our minds to wander off course when engaging in an activity that requires mental focus. We are all different in our capabilities in this regard. But it is within our ability to mitigate the tendency of our animal brains to get distracted. Formal prayer with printed words helps us to do this.

At a minimum, I suggest starting the day with the Sign of the Cross and offering the day to the Lord, and saying a prayer before going to sleep. Brick by brick you can build up your personal "rule" of prayer. This will inevitably lead us closer to God, break the hold of sin on our souls, and allow us to see things as they truly are. Greater clarity in apprehending underlying reality comes with the grace that the Lord will shower on us as a result of us turning to Him.

Holy Images and Objects

A powerful supplement to our verbal prayers is the use of holy images and objects. There are any number of readily available and theologically Orthodox icons, paintings, and statues of Christ, Mary, and St. Jude. We would do well to acquire some of them and to get them blessed by a priest. I highly recommend having a decent collection of blessed holy art in your home; it is almost necessary for a proper Christian prayer life.

What about the First Commandment, with its strict divine injunction against any graven images or made likenesses? "I am the LORD your God… You shall have no other gods before me. You shall not make for yourself a graven image, or any likeness of anything" (Dt 5:6-8). This law of God applies just as much now as at any time. But when we are using holy images and objects, *we are NOT worshipping them.*

Indeed, "the honor rendered to an image passes to its prototype," and "whoever venerates an image venerates the person portrayed in it." The honor paid to sacred images is a "respectful veneration," not the adoration due to God alone. (CCC 2132)

We humans are physical creatures, members of the Animal Kingdom who are affected mentally and emotionally by the sensory input our brains receive. Praying before an icon or other holy image of St. Jude anchors our attention in a manner similar to how the printed text of prayers guides and directs the articulation of our innermost longings.

If you are lucky enough to get a chance to venerate a relic of Jude Thaddeus at a shrine, that would be awesome. St. Jude holy oil can be ordered from some shrines. And, St. Jude candles are widely available in a variety of shops, including many supermarkets.

It is crucial to keep in mind that this is not magic or the occult; we want to squash any superstitious ideas. The power of the objects and images to assist us comes from God giving His grace to us in response to our faith. During Jesus' earthly ministry, people "begged him that they might touch even the fringe of his garment; and as many as touched it were made well" (Mk 6:56). The fringe of His garment was just cloth. The healing power came from Christ Himself, working through a created object in response to the people's faith. It's the same today and will be every day till kingdom come.

All Roads Lead To Calvary

All roads lead to and from the Cross of Christ. It is the aperture through which one must travel in order to gain life; it is also the fountain from which springs the life that sustains us forward. It's what gives Jude Thaddeus the ability to help us in our need. Every grace we receive is made possible by the bloody sacrifice of Jesus on the Cross. It is the decisive event in the history of the human race.

And, it is here with us now. Literally. This is where the Christian service known as the "Mass" comes in. It is also known as the "Divine Liturgy" or "Holy Qurbana." What distinguishes this service from those of non-Catholic congregations is:

1) It is the Eucharistic sacrifice – in its substance it is the actual sacrifice of Jesus Christ on the Cross, breaching the humanly impenetrable borders of time and locality in order to reach into any time or place wherein the priests of the Holy Church operate.

2) It is in full communion with the visible head of the Church on Earth, the Pope of Rome, which puts those who are lawfully participat-

ing into full communion with the invisible and eternal head of the Church, Jesus Christ.

So you see, the Mass is far more than a get-together for prayer and listening to the reading of scripture. Don't get me wrong, there is plenty of good accomplished by communal prayer and Bible reading. In fact, if you can get together with enough like-minded people, I highly, *highly* encourage it.

The Divine Liturgy, though, is above any other kind of prayer because it is the actual sacrifice of Christ on the Cross at Calvary. It requires true faith, because we do not see things as they actually are. Congregants can see other congregants, the altar, and religious art; they can smell the incense; they can hear the singing, chanting, and reading. But God is requiring us to believe that what is actually going on is the meeting of heaven and earth, and to trust Him that the full reality of the Mass will be revealed to us in the next life.

My point in bringing up the Liturgy is that the **most effective way** to empower your prayers to St. Jude Thaddeus is to tap into the source, Jesus Christ. The means by which Christ makes His grace available to us is His sacrifice on the Cross. In a manner that transcends the wildest imaginations of science fiction authors, He has allowed us the privilege of travelling through time and space by joining Him at Calvary and in heaven. That is to say, He has given us the Divine Liturgy, the Holy Mass.

Well then, *what* is it that we should do?

1) **Make ourselves worthy.** Strictly speaking, we can never be worthy. But at least we can come to Him in a manner that does not invite extra judgement and condemnation on ourselves. If you are not in the

Catholic Church, I encourage you to become a member of the body of Christ. If you are already in full communion with the Pope of Rome, let's take advantage of the sanctifying grace that Jesus gives us to cleanse our souls in the Sacrament of Confession. Let's emphasize to ourselves the importance of avoiding sin, and praise Christ God for the gift of His flesh and blood in Holy Communion.

2) **Attend ourselves.** Christ desires to feed His sheep through His Church (Jn 21:15-17). So we need to follow through and physically attend the primary means by which He does so. If we already do attend, we can always do so with greater fervor.

I do wish to tack on a little warning about numbers and quantity. Each individual Mass is literally *infinite*. One hundred Masses are not better than one in their substance. Each Liturgy is a temporal instantiation of an eternal reality. The reason for the obligatory Sunday Mass for Catholics and for the utility of multiple Masses being said for particular intentions is *our* limitations, not that of the Divine Liturgy. The limitations stemming from our fallen human condition make it difficult to open our souls to His grace. But we *can* do it – what it might take is for us to open ourselves to Him incrementally, bit by bit. The more we do so the more He will flood our souls with His grace.

3) **Have Masses said for our intentions.**

a) In Petition – Because it is Jesus Christ at Calvary who is on the altar at the Divine Liturgy, it is the greatest of all prayers. You do not even have to be in attendance yourself to get a Mass said for your intentions, so take advantage of this magnificent privilege. Contact the shrines listed in Chapter 4 and have them offer the Eucharistic sacrifice on your behalf. They will be happy to help – that's what they're there for!

b) In Thanksgiving – There is no greater thanksgiving than the Eucharistic sacrifice, the Mass. Indeed, *Eucharist* is from the Greek word for "thanksgiving," and Jude/Judas/Judah/Jew comes from the Hebrew word for "thanksgiving." The semantic-symbolic connection is profound.

4) **Personal Prayer.** The Liturgy (a.k.a. Christ crucified) is the source of every grace, but what are we supposed to do when we are not in church? Personal prayer is the answer to this question. Popular devotions such as the St. Jude Thaddeus devotion "extend the liturgical life of the Church"; they "are in some way derived from it [*the sacred liturgy*] and lead people to it" (CCC 1675). St. Jude thus helps us tap into the vein of Jesus' infinite love and mercy. His aid to us delivers blessing to our unique life circumstances, blessings which are ultimately derived from the Eucharist (a.k.a. Jesus Christ).

What Is Going On With St. Jude When I Pray To Him?

While you are praying on earth, St. Jude is seconding your prayer in heaven. It is the same as if you were to ask a friend on earth to pray for your intentions. The main difference is that the prayers of St. Jude Thaddeus are far more powerful than those of any of us sinners here on earth. He has been purified by his life of service to the Gospel of his God and kinsman, Jesus Christ. He was granted the special privilege of bringing "visible and speedy help where help is almost despaired of."

Concerning the saints, the Church teaches us that "they contemplate God, praise him and constantly care for those whom they have left on earth" (CCC 2683), "so by their fraternal concern is our weakness greatly helped" (CCC 956). This is what Jude is doing behind the scenes. He is working overtime (so to speak) to get from God the best possible outcome to our petitions.

A good piece of advice: Please do not expect that you will know exactly how the will of God will play out in your life! Even if our request is being granted, there is a very good chance that it will be in an unexpected manner. I have had this happen to me on more occasions than I can count.

Our life is designed in such a way as to afford us the very best possible chance of being rewarded the Paradise described earlier in this chapter. However, the operative factor, and the thing we actually control, is our free will. After all, that's why it's called "free" will.

We have to *choose* to avail ourselves of the opportunities that God provides to us. When we call upon St. Jude Thaddeus, we can be confident that we have hit upon a spiritual treasure of heavenly help.

The really cool thing about the saints in heaven is that they do not abandon us. They have no real incentive to help us except for their pure selfless love, their *caritas* or "charity." They already have everything they could possibly need or desire. St. Jude is set; he has no need to bother with us on earth. Yet, the very thing that got him to a high position in heaven – a life lived in service to his burning, passionate love for Christ – is the very thing that causes him to continue helping us on earth.

He sees Christ in each of us, so it only stands to reason that someone who sees the Truth with such clarity would act with mercy towards those who need it the most. Indeed, he beckons all of us who call upon him to adopt the same attitude. All the faithful, both the saints in heaven and us pilgrims on earth are in an interconnected network of prayer.

Jude Thaddeus is supporting us from his position of glory just as we on earth are helping each other get through this "Valley of Tears."

The Church speaks of this prayerful communion with the saints:

... that by this devotion to the exercise of fraternal charity the union of the whole Church in the Spirit may be strengthened. Exactly as our Christian communion among our fellow pilgrims brings us closer to Christ, so our communion with the saints joins us to Christ, from whom as from its fountain and head issues all grace (CCC 957).

Just as we pray to Jude and he prays for us, so also we pray for others and they pray for us, and we all move closer to Christ, the fulfillment of every human destiny.

4

Where

Where can we pray to St. Jude?

The quick answer is, drum roll please … *anywhere!*

Home, Work, School, Driving, Shopping, Gym, Beach, Woods…

We can pray to him anywhere we happen to be in the world. However it is that we spend the days of our lives, we can incorporate some regularity into our patterns of prayer. Such regularity does not rule our spontaneous prayer in response to a specific need or inspiration. It's simply that regularity of practice serves as a solid structure upon which to flesh out our response to the dynamic situations that life inevitably throws in our direction. Good habits build virtue, and in turn, virtue allows us to handle challenges more effectively.

Most people tend to spend the greater part of their day at home, at work, and in transit. Personally, I like to pray formal, memorized devotions such as the Rosary when I'm traveling. I tend to do a lot of driving, so prayer in the serenity of a long drive tends to center my mind and spirit. I have to give credit to the actor Martin Sheen for inspiring this idea.

When many of today's God-fearing people are at home or at work, their duties tend to keep them busy so that they cannot regularly schedule prayer during these times. So, they wait for gaps in the action. They use longer gaps to recite formally worded invocations, and shorter ones to turn their minds and hearts to shorter utterances.

In addition, any number of memorized scripture verses or other holy sayings can pop into their heads during the course of the day, either in response to some here-and-now situation or while lost in some mental meandering. These, too, are a form of prayer.

Prayer practices such as those I just described exemplify how to adapt the continual conversation with heaven to a life *in* the world, but not *of* it. There is certainly no requirement to follow the exact pattern laid out above; you can do it your own way in your own life. The **central idea** is to **keep talking** to God and to the angels and saints, His friends. By doing so, you will be following the example and command of Christ and His Apostles (Mk 1:35; Lk 6:12; Lk 18:1; 1 Thes 5:17). In turn, the Lord will love you in a particularly special way: "If a man loves me, he will keep my word and my Father will love him, and we will come to him and make our home with him" (Jn 14:23 – this verse, by the way, is part of our Lord's response to Jude's question at the Last Supper, covered more fully below).

Praying, my dear friends, is something we can do **wherever** we are.

Church

While we can and should pray anywhere, the fact remains that certain places are just better for this purpose. "The choice of a favorable place is not a matter of indifference for true prayer" (CCC 2691). **Where** we pray matters. So while we can and should pray at home, work, and everywhere we are in the course of our daily lives, we should also make a determined effort to pray in certain locations that are blessed in a more special way. These places are just holier than other places because they have been consecrated for a holy purpose.

At the top of the list of holy places are churches. A Catholic church in which Christ Himself lives and in which the Eucharistic sacrifice is offered on the altar is certainly the holiest of holy places. The big-C Church teaches that a little-c church is the most appropriate place for prayer above all others (CCC 2696). It is also, of course, "the proper place for liturgical prayer for the parish community" and "the privileged place for adoration of the real presence of Christ in the Blessed Sacrament" (CCC 2691).

But please don't allow the sublime majesty of the house of God scare you off when it comes to praying for your personal intentions through a devotion of popular piety. You can certainly pray to St. Jude in the physical building in which heaven and earth meet. Christ will not mind you invoking one of His proven servants, and the benefits of being in the Lord's *physical* presence while doing so are incalculable.

Of course, in the context of the liturgical worship for which churches are the primary setting, the prayers of the congregation are geared towards the ultimate goal of eternal salvation. This is the most important thing, and taking part in the Liturgy lifts our souls to heaven.

But whether we are praying with the community in Liturgy or by ourselves when the church is empty, the anxiety of a personal issue for which we are praying can intrude on our attentiveness to the big-picture salvation of the world. So by all means, invoke St. Jude in church! He is God's first responder for dealing with brush fires in our lives so that our hearts and minds can be freed to contemplate the transcendent mysteries of the Lord.

WARNING about receiving the Eucharist: By all means, attend Mass on Sunday and whenever you can. *But,* if you have been away from regular Catholic worship, *please* ask a priest before ever partaking of Holy Communion – there are some very specific rules and we do not want to be guilty of sacrilege!

Shrines

An extremely ancient and holy Christian practice is that of pilgrimage, the visiting of particular holy sites, especially at specific times designated for sacred commemorations. The Church teaches us that, "pilgrimages evoke our earthly journey toward heaven and are traditionally very special occasions for renewal in prayer. For pilgrims seeking living water, shrines are special places for living the forms of Christian prayer 'in Church'" (CCC 2691).

Below is a list of holy places associated with St. Jude. It is not exhaustive (my apologies to any shrines that I overlooked), but it is a great place to start. These shrines exist to bring St. Jude Thaddeus to the world.

If you are fortunate enough to be able to make a pilgrimage to one of these shrines, that's awesome. By all means, show your devotion to God's first responder. While you're there, I'd be personally grateful for any prayers you might throw in for me and my family; likewise, I am praying for you and your family – we're all in this together!

If you are not able to make the pilgrimage, you can still contact the shrines and have prayers said for your intentions. As we went over in the last chapter, you can get Masses said for your petition. The Holy Mass, the Divine Liturgy, is not just the greatest of all prayers, but the meeting of heaven and Earth. If we and our intentions are being prayed for at Liturgy, we can rest assured and confident in God's infinite power, mercy, and care for us.

Starter List of St. Jude's Holy Places

Here are some places that are important to the St. Jude devotion. Most of these are great places to reach out to if you wish to have Masses said for your petitions, or to donate to in order to help these servants of God continue in their holy work.

CHILE
Location: Santiago; La Basílica del Corazón de María
Name: Santuario San Judas Tadeo
Run by: Missionary Sons of the Immaculate Heart of Mary (CMF, the Claretians)
Website: sanjudas.cl

INDIA
Location: Jhansi, Madhya Pradesh
Name: St. Jude's Shrine
Run by: Diocese of Jhansi (Latin Rite)
Website: stjudeshrinejhansi.org

Location: Koothattukulam, Kerala; Holy Family Church
Name: St. Jude Shrine
Run by: Syro-Malabar Catholic Church
Website: stjudekoothattukulam.org

MEXICO

Location: Cuauhtémoc, Mexico City; El Templo de San Hipólito
Name: El Santuario de San Judas Tadeo
Run by: Missionary Sons of the Immaculate Heart of Mary (CMF, the Claretians)
Website: claretianos.mx

PHILIPPINES

Location: San Miguel, Manila
Name: National Shrine of St. Jude Thaddeus
Run by: Society of the Divine Word (SVD, the Divine Word Missionaries)
Website: stjudemanila.com

UNITED STATES

Location: Baltimore, Maryland; former St. John the Baptist Church
Name: St. Jude Shrine
Run by: Society of the Catholic Apostolate (SAC, the Pallottines)
Website: stjudeshrine.org

Location: Chicago, Illinois; Church of St. Pius V
Name: Dominican Shrine of St. Jude Thaddeus
Run by: Order of Preachers (OP, the Dominicans)
Website: the-shrine.org

Location: Chicago, Illinois; Our Lady of Guadalupe Church
Name: National Shrine of St. Jude
Run by: Missionary Sons of the Immaculate Heart of Mary (CMF, the Claretians)
Website: shrineofstjude.org

Location: Garrison, New York
Name: Graymoor: The Holy Mountain
Run by: Franciscan Friars of the Atonement
Website: atonementfriars.org/st-jude-monthly

Location: Memphis, Tennessee
Name: St. Jude Children's Research Hospital
Run by: American Lebanese Syrian Associated Charities (ALSAC)
Website: stjude.org

Location: Mount Vernon, New York
Name: Franciscan Mission Associates
Run by: Order of Friars Minor (OFM, the Franciscans)
Website: franciscanmissionassoc.org/prayer-requests/devotional-saints/st-jude

Location: New Orleans, Louisiana; Our Lady of Guadalupe Church
Name: International Shrine of St. Jude
Run by: Missionary Oblates of Mary Immaculate (OMI)
Website: judeshrine.com

Location: New York, New York; Church of St. Catherine of Siena
Name: Dominican Shrine of St. Jude
Run by: Order of Preachers (OP, the Dominicans)
Website: jude.parish.opeast.org

Location: San Francisco, California; St. Dominic's Church
Name: Shrine of St. Jude Thaddeus
Run by: Order of Preachers (OP, the Dominicans)
Website: stjude-shrine.org

Location: Washington, District of Colombia; St. Dominic's Church
Name: Rosary Shrine of St. Jude
Run by: Order of Preachers (OP, the Dominicans)
Website: rosaryshrineofstjude.org

Location: Waterford, Connecticut; St. Ann's Church
Name: St. Jude Shrine
Run by: Melkite Greek-Catholic Church
Website: stannmelkitechurch.org

Where in the World...

Where in the world is the St. Jude Thaddeus devotion practiced?

Well, we get some ideas by looking at the preceding list. But wait, there's more.

As Jesus was about to ascend back to His Father, forty days after He rose from the dead, He told Jude and the gathered Apostles, "You shall receive power when the Holy Spirit has come upon you; and you shall be my witnesses in Jerusalem and in all Judea and Samaria and to the end of the earth" (Acts 1:8).

This was the answer to a question Jude asked at the Last Supper!

The Gospel of John relates St. Jude's only spoken line in the Gospels, which is this question he addressed to the Lord:

Judas (not Iscariot) said to him, 'Lord, how is it that you will manifest yourself to us, and not to the world?' Jesus answered him, 'If a man loves me, he will keep my word and my Father will love him, and we will come to him and make our home with him. ... the Counselor, the Holy Spirit whom the Father will send in my name, he will teach you all things, and bring to your remembrance all that I have said to you. (Jn 14:22-23, 26).

Now it was clear. Once He sent His Holy Spirit, Christ would manifest to man through His word, which was to be communicated by the Apostles and their successors "to the end of the earth."

Jesus' answer to Jude might have seemed cryptic at the Last Supper – the answer is not an obvious fit to the question. But if there was any lingering uncertainty in any of the Apostles' minds, the Lord addressed it again in the very last words He spoke on Earth before He permanently disappeared from view.

It was up to Jude Thaddeus to manifest Christ to the end of the earth. And so, that's what he did.

Yes, of course, the other Apostles and disciples were to do the same. But Christians will take it as their personal responsibility to do everything in their own power to spread the Gospel in their own way. For Jude, this meant an active preaching ministry.

It is ironic that St. Jude the Apostle was ever known as the unknown or forgotten saint, because his influence is actually quite ancient and deep. It is impossible to reconstruct his exact missionary travels in the way we can with St. Paul. However, the overwhelming weight of available evidence indicates that he covered an area to the north and east of the land of Israel.

The following are the main known areas of his missionary activity (he is usually called Thaddeus in these missionary contexts):

Edessa – This was an Aramaic-speaking city-state in what is now south-east Turkey. It was a major center of the early Church and straddled the border of the Roman and Persian Empires for centuries, frequently changing hands. It was here that Jude Thaddeus made his most distinctive contribution to the early growth of the Church. When he cured King Abgar with the burial shroud of Christ, he not only laid the foundation of his own patronage of hopeless causes, but also set a precedent for the Christian use of holy images. Millenia of sacred art has been the result.

Armenia – The first nation in the world to make Christianity its official religion, back in the year 301. A couple of centuries before this, the seed of the Church was planted there by Thaddeus and his fellow Apostle Bartholomew. They were both reputed to have been martyred in Armenia. And if it's true that the blood of the martyrs is the seed of the Church, they certainly planted their seed deeply. The Armenians have beaten all the odds to survive to this day as a distinct people. The fact that their national patron is also the patron of lost causes and desperate difficulties is likely no small part of their improbable success.

Mesopotamia and Persia – Aside from the more specific locales above, Jude Thaddeus is also associated with missionary activity in the territories covered by the modern countries of Iraq and Iran. His main missionary associate from among the Twelve seems to have been St. Thomas, who is also associated with this region. St. Thaddeus was assisted in this endeavor by his disciple St. Mari, who took over the mantle of evangelization from his mentor just as Elisha did from Elijah (1 Kgs 19:15-19). Some accounts say he was martyred in Persia along with St. Simon the Zealot.

Lebanon/Libya – There are also some accounts that St. Jude was martyred in Beirut, Lebanon. St. Paulinus of Nola also mentions that he preached in Libya; while this is certainly possible, it is more likely a confusion with the phonetically similar *Lebanon*. Whether or not he was historically in Libya, Thaddeus was certainly a popular saint in Christian Africa. One of the earliest historical references to St. Jude Thaddeus is by St. Clement of Alexandria, Egypt, and the story of him curing King Abgar with the image of Christ was popular not only in Greek, but in Coptic (Egyptian) and Ge'ez (Ethiopian) versions.

Jude Thaddeus wrote the core of the Eucharistic Liturgy used in the ancient Church of the East, the modern Catholic reflexes of which are the Chaldean and Syro-Malabar Churches. As of the early 21st Century, the only dense concentrations of these Christian populations in their ancient territories are around the city of Mosul in northern Iraq and in the southern Indian region of Malabar. The faithful in Mesopotamia recently suffered a particularly severe genocidal persecution under the Islamic State of Iraq and Syria (ISIS). The fact that the community survived at all is a testament to the power of Christ and the loving, protective intercession of St. Thaddeus. If the blood of the martyrs is the seed of the Church, let's pray that Jesus will mercifully allow the Chaldean Church, so dearly loved by St. Jude Thaddeus, to recover from the horror of persecution and to revive its evangelistic vigor.

Historically, the Church of the East stretched eastwards from Edessa (in modern Turkey) through Mesopotamia, Persia, and Afghanistan, after which it branched off south through India and north through central Asia into China.

Thaddeus truly had some reach!

In the Christian west, the influence of our Apostle was subtle yet profound. We saw in the last chapter how Jude Thaddeus bringing the burial shroud of the Lord to Edessa and curing King Abgar with it was the starting point of his subsequent patronage of the desperate and hopeless. But we also owe a centuries long flourishing of religious art in part to St. Jude. Stories of Jude Thaddeus bringing the burial shroud of Christ to Edessa were revived in the 8th and 9th centuries during the Iconoclast controversies.

The logical conclusion drawn by the Church during this era, under the guidance of the Holy Spirit, was that since the Son of God left us His physical image, it was a good and holy thing to depict Him and other holy subjects in art. Eastern and western European art developed on different paths after this, but they both go back to the doctrine articulated at the Seventh Ecumenical Council of the Catholic Church (Nicea II, held in 767) that, "the honor rendered to an image passes to its prototype" (CCC 2132). Because it was he who transported and protected the burial shroud of Christ, it is to St. Jude Thaddeus that we owe a large measure of thanks for the many positive outcomes that resulted from its preservation.

By the way, this cloth, known as the Mandylion, was eventually transported from Edessa to Constantinople. It thus escaped the clutches of the Saracens (Muslims), thanks be to God. It was then transported to France in the 13th century. This time, it was a criminal theft by westerners of the Fourth Crusade. However, the results of this evil act turned out to be providential in regard to the shroud. This is because Constantinople also eventually fell to the Saracens, in 1453 – thanks be to God for saving the relic again! The Mandylion was transported from France to Italy in 1578, where it has remained, and has since been known as the Holy Shroud of Turin.

Now, Jude Thaddeus himself was the subject of minor devotion in the west throughout the centuries of the second millennium. He was called upon by St. Bernard of Clairvaux, France (12th century), St. Birgitta of Sweden (14th century), and Pope Paul III (16th century). A large portion of his relics are housed in St. Peter's Basilica in Rome.

His devotion spread westward to the New World with the Spanish Empire. Writer Brian Morgan relates that, "in the Sutro Library in California, there rests a treasure dating back to 1702. It is a worn, but precious sixteen-page Spanish novena to Saint Jude."[6] No later than the early 19th century Jude Thaddeus was being invoked as the patron of the desperate and the hopeless, as is clear in the Latin *Little Office of St. Jude (Officium Parvum)* which was published in 1826. By 1911, the *cultus* was sufficiently popular for a shrine to the Apostle to be opened in Santiago, Chile.

As mentioned, the real breakthrough happened in 1929, in the Church of Our Lady of Guadalupe in Chicago. This was a parish for Mexican immigrants run by the Claretian order. A statue and shrine of the hitherto obscure St. Jude caught on in a massive, never-before-seen wave of popularity. The language barrier was penetrated, and Jude found enthusiastic adherents in the children of immigrants from Ireland, Italy, and eastern Europe.

Nobody understood exactly why St. Jude attracted such sudden attention; this was at the tail end of the Roaring Twenties, so Americans were generally prosperous. Those of a pious mindset would see the hand of God at work, giving the faithful a spiritual tool to fight the physical, financial, and emotional challenges of the Great Depression which was about to hit. And in fact, devotion to St. Jude "went viral," so to speak, among American Catholics during the 1930's and into World War II. In tandem with his religious role, he joined the pantheon of early-mid 20th century American *cultural* heroes such as Superman, the Lone Ranger, and Buck Rogers.

Don't get me wrong, there are some real gems in American popular culture (yes, there is also a lot of trash, but we're not talking about that right now). Superman, in particular, is a lifelong favorite of mine. But there is something very different about Jude, and that is that he is a **real** and ancient Christian saint. Unlike the fictional Superman, the powers of St. Jude Thaddeus are **true** and documented.

The geographical span of this revived devotion was not confined to America. Due to the disproportional influence of the United States as the world's only free superpower, anything American enjoyed a certain enhanced prestige in the decades after World War II. This included matters pertaining to geopolitics, military affairs, and cultural influence – the latter most prominently exemplified by Hollywood and Rock and Roll.

Positive religious influence was also a part of this trend, and one of the great gifts of the American Church to the world was the devotion to St. Jude Thaddeus. This is only to say that the tremendous popularity he enjoyed in the U.S. filtered to other parts of the world through something of a cultural osmosis, making its way to places as diverse as Australia, the Philippines, and Ireland.

Yes, Ireland – from the west St. Jude filtered back east to parts of the Old World with strong links to America. My grandfather, Séamus Ó Fianghusa (James Fennessy) from Limerick City in Ireland, was a devotee of Jude Thaddeus. In the far northwest of Ireland, the community of Oileán Thoraigh (Tory Island) has historically been sufficiently remote to protect its Irish linguistic heritage and ancient cultural practices. But even here, the new-ancient saint found his way. Out of less than dozen fishing motor boats owned by islandmen in the mid-20th century, one was named *Saint Pius and Saint Jude*.[7]

The outward filtration affected the New World as well. We saw that the St. Jude devotion was carried to the U.S. by Mexican immigrants who planted roots in Chicago. Like a sea-swell splashing backwards after impacting a rock on the shore, it reverberated back to Mexico in the mid-20th century. *San Judas Tadeo* catapulted to an unparalleled popularity and has maintained his prominence in the consciousness of the Mexican faithful. After the Virgin of Guadalupe, he is now the most venerated saint in Mexico.

Back in the States, Jude acquired something of a celebrity status. The actor and comedian Danny Thomas and his founding of St. Jude Children's Research Hospital had some part in this. I might also make mention of another actor of Lebanese background, Jamie Farr. When he was struggling to make it in his chosen profession he turned to St. Jude. He then caught his big break when he landed a role playing St. Jude in a movie! You can't make this up. Jamie later went on to great success on the television series *M*A*S*H* as the quirky Corporal Clinger.

Celebrities were one thing. But the bigger factor in building the high reputation and prestige of the St. Jude Thaddeus devotion was a **track record of successful and documented intercession, often with amazing or even miraculous results**.

Despite his ancient pedigree, the very thing that was advantageous to his *cultus* or public devotion catching on in the U.S. was that he had no perceivable Old World ties that boxed him into insular clannishness. Other saints whose devotions were brought over to America from Europe were connected, let's say, to particular villages in southern Italy. Jude, however, was a "generalist" as scholar Robert Orsi put it,[8] and was something of a blank slate to Americans when his devotion took off in 1929. His domain of patronage was rather broad, covering **desperate** difficulties, **hopeless** cases, **impossible** situations, and **lost causes.** These categories have a wide scope, and their subjective nature form a contrast to the sharply delineated boundaries of patronage associated with Old World favorites.

St. Jude Thaddeus is not just a generalist in terms of his patronage, but as a universal saint of the One, Holy, Catholic, and Apostolic Church. He ties together the extremities of the Christian experience. On the one hand, his influence stretched to the furthest eastern reaches of the Church's missionary activity in the Old World from ancient times. On the other hand, he is venerated in a devotion that revolutionized popular piety in recent times, a devotion which spread out from one of the newest countries on earth, located in the New World of the Far West.

More than any other saint I am aware of, he epitomizes the aphorism the Son of God gave us, that "many that are first will be last, and last first" (Mk 10:31).

Where is St. Jude Thaddeus Right Now?

In heaven with God, of course! His soul is in the midst of bliss that will never end. As a result of his perfected charity, his concern is that we join him. He lived on earth two millennia ago, we never met him, and yet he knows us better than our dearest friends and family do. And we too, even here on earth, can feel like we know him personally. This theme of personal affection and intimacy is a consistent and pervasive trait of the devotion to St. Jude.

Question: If St. Jude is in heaven and heaven is where God is, where exactly is this "heaven" – where is God?

Answer: He is "everywhere," so to speak, as we are told in one of the first entries in the old Baltimore Catechism.

60

The paradise of heaven is an indescribable state of existence. It is *literally* **eternal**, unconstrained by time and space. Please keep in mind that spatial concepts encoded in human language do not do justice to the reality of heaven. Strictly speaking, the eternal life of the "beatific vision" cannot be constricted in its substance by earthly concepts of place. So, when we say something like "He is *in* heaven," we are using a linguistic workaround to describe what's really going on. This is something to keep in mind when utilizing the limited tools of our expressive capability.

St. Jude's body was martyred in the 1st century A.D. It has since mostly decomposed, like all our bodies will. However, preserved pieces of his body are venerated as relics in the various locations consecrated to him – look back at the list of shrines. For instance, the Dominican Shrine in Chicago has a big piece of the Apostle's wrist bone.[9]

This is all a temporary situation. At the resurrection of the dead at the end of history, his body will be reconstituted and then reunited with his soul. That is certainly an appropriate reward for the Apostle responsible for saving the premier relic of the Resurrection of Christ (the Mandylion/Holy Shroud of Turin).

And you know what else? You and I will be there too, reunited with our bodies on the last day. If we follow the path Jude Thaddeus laid out for us with his life and teachings, we will follow him to join Christ in eternal glory.

5

When

The big question here is **when** is it appropriate to invoke St. Jude Thaddeus? In what situations, and what time of day or year?

I hope it's clear at this point that we can call upon him at any time. While a Christian should be praying to God every day, we do not have to pray to St. Jude every day. We certainly *can* pray to him every day though; I do, and I recommend it.

However, if you are going to pray regularly at all, my advice is to start with the basic Christian prayers in Appendix B. The first place goes to God, then to His mother, and then to angels and saints.

On the other hand, Jude Thaddeus can be the gateway to Christ for many. He has taken the role of heavenly confidant for multitudes through the decades, even centuries. And so, if your devotion to our saint leads you to end up conversing with Jude more than with any other holy being, Christ our Lord is pleased.

The most important thing to get going is to start a conversation with heaven and to *keep* it going. In order to give our prayers a certain regularity or daily rhythm, it is good to look at some basic and time-tested Christian prayer customs. Here are some suggestions to start:

- Start the day with the Sign of the Cross.
- Give thanks to God for meals.
- Say good-night to God.

If you master these first three, here are a couple more simple practices to adopt:

- Pray at the beginning and/or end of an activity.
- Pray during the 3pm hour, the hour Christ died on the Cross.

Feast Days of Jude Thaddeus the Apostle

Certain days of the year are specially dedicated to Jude Thaddeus. These are usually called "feast days." Whether or not we are invoking him for a particular intention around the time of these dates, it can only benefit us to pay him special respect in our prayers for that day. The following are his principal feasts:

5th Sunday of Easter (most frequently around early May) – The great feast of Mar Addai Sleeha (St. Thaddeus the Apostle) in the Chaldean and Syro-Malabar Catholic Churches, whose traditional geographic territories were evangelized by the Apostle himself (Mesopotamia and Persia; India has used the Liturgy attributed to him from the earliest days).

June 19 – Byzantine Rite feast under the name "St. Jude the Apostle."

August 21 – Byzantine Rite feast under the name "St. Thaddeus of Edessa."

September 28 – Latin Rite feast, shared with St. Simon the Zealot.

The Armenian feast of St. Thaddeus the Apostle generally falls mid-late July. The saints' feasts days in the Armenian Church are moveable, that is, they are not on the exact same date every year.

It is interesting to note that Jude's various feast days are packed into the middle of the year, in a five-month span from May-September. I think it's pretty cool that we have so many opportunities to honor him in a particularly special way through the celebration of his feast days. And, the celebration of these days allows us to have an extra focus for holiness during a chunk of the year that lies outside of the periods dominated by the great holy feasts of Christmas and Easter.

The Infinite Well

A fear has historically been expressed by many devotees of St. Jude that makes them reluctant to invoke him except in the most extreme difficulties. This is understandable, because nobody wants to be the boy who cried, "Wolf!"

It is important to point out that **the power of St. Jude's prayers do not run out**. The merit that he accumulated on Earth is permanent. He truly acquired the treasure in heaven that Jesus told us about (Mt 6:20).

This is wonderful for us in two ways. One, we can pray with confidence that Jude's intercession is an inexhaustible source of heavenly aid. It will *never* run out. The other is that he shows us that our own work for God's glory will last forever if we make it past the finish line. In fact, it is the only thing we work for that will actually last. St. Jude is no different from us in his nature – he walked the Earth as a fallible, flesh and blood human. Yet, his glory and power last forever because of the life he led for the only Lord and Master, Jesus Christ.

A similarly awesome destiny awaits us if we live by the Gospel, until the very end, just like Jude did.

Because his power from God has no actual limit, everyone could stand to benefit from calling upon his assistance. If every single person on Earth accepted the Gospel and was baptized into the Catholic Church, as our Father earnestly desires, the help of St. Jude Thaddeus would be just as strong. There is no "diluting" it: no such thing exists.

So if you only call upon our great advocate Jude in emergency situations, that's just fine. That's what he's there for. He is God's own emergency responder and he loves to help us. But you can also speak to him on a daily basis as a trusted confidant; many do this, and it is highly commendable.

Strength When We Need It

Below we will go over some of the situations that are most suitable for calling on St. Jude for help.

First, let's remind ourselves of what exactly his domain is – St. Jude Thaddeus is a *GENERAL PURPOSE* EMERGENCY SERVICE SAINT. His intercession is particularly effective for **desperate** difficulties, **hopeless** cases, **impossible** situations, and **lost causes**.

These are somewhat broad categories. What counts as "desperate" or "hopeless" is quite subjective, and depends to some extent on a given individual's emotional constitution.

That's okay!

That actually allows us greater flexibility in approaching St. Jude because we can present to him our subjective internal state and not rely on impersonal metrics. He understands. He cares. Jude actually *gets* you.

Take a look at this list, which is nearly identical to the lists in Chapter 1. It will remind us about **when** we should invoke St. Jude Thaddeus:

- Medical crises, ailments, incurable diseases
- Poverty, financial relief and success
- Employment and careers
- Academic success
- Legal issues
- Addiction
- Family turmoil and distress
- Depression, overwhelming stress, general emotional distress
- Devilry or demonic oppression
- Purity and chastity
- Courting, dating, looking to meet someone special
- Getting pregnant
- Safe childbirth
- Animal welfare

Now is this pretty comprehensive or what?

I do wish to note that St. Jude is especially helpful in dealing with matters of chastity and matters of romantic love. These two matters are polar opposites in the eyes of the world, but faithful Christians understand they are two sides of the same coin.

Chastity is nothing less than the proper sexuality for one's state in life. The key is to have a *clean heart*. A certain few are chosen for celibacy; one of these was St. Bernard (d. 1153), who credited St. Jude with preserving his purity. Jude himself came down very hard on sexual libertines, as the entirety of his biblical letter demonstrates. But marital union was created and blessed by God, and Jude Thaddeus himself was a married man with children. In fact, an early tradition says that he was the one getting married at Cana when Jesus worked his first public miracle (Jn 2:1-11).

The Challenge of Faith

Whatever issue you are bringing to heaven's attention, be assured that God knows, understands, and deeply cares. Jesus tells us that "your Father knows what you need before you ask him" (Mt 6:8).

But then, one might protest, what is the use of praying if God knows already?

Because, He wants us to *come to Him in faith.*

Those in distress who feel impending despair but then call on St. Jude do have to confront a paradoxical challenge: they are feeling hopeless, but must have faith at the same time. Nobody who feels this way is alone, because this has been the challenge for the faithful Jew and then Christian since time immemorial! These faithful ones who have already passed the test are in heaven praying for us, especially if we call on them. And powerful St. Jude will be at the head of this pack if you make him your special patron.

On top of it all, and I'm saying it again to drive home this truth, your Father knows your needs and will richly reward your perseverance in faith.

When Will St. Jude Answer Us?

St. Jude hears us right away, there is no doubt about that. But as far as the question of **when** he will answer our prayer, it's the same answer to the question of when we can call upon him: *any time*. It could be immediate, or it could take some time. Or maybe – brace yourself – it might never quite turn out how you want it to.

But don't worry – if we make it to the end of our lives as faithful Christians, there is *nothing* that will not be better in the eternal life to come! Knowing this is a perpetual source of comfort even in the sticky here-and-now situations that St. Jude is so famous for helping us out of.

According to the Lord's merciful providence, people who have a shaky faith might have their petitions answered in a spectacular and speedy manner, while those with a great faith might have their petition granted only after years of petitioning. On the other hand, one with a weaker faith might not have their request granted until they open themselves more to the Gospel, while someone who lives with the Gospel always close to their heart will get an immediate and powerful response.

The path that Christ lays out for each individual one of us is the same, in that we are to go to the Father through Him. This is a universal truth, even though our individual lives are unique. I urge everyone who turns to St. Jude to keep this in mind when thinking about the seemingly unequal distribution of blessings.

The blessings of heaven are for the Lord God to distribute, His alone. In the parable of the vineyard (Lk 20:1-16), the master of the vineyard says to one of his workers who is complaining about perceived inequality, "Am I not allowed to do what I choose with what belongs to me?" God is the ultimate in fairness and compassion. Thus, no matter how unjust things appear, be rest assured that everything will be okay if we are steadfast in the Gospel to the end.

The timing of **when** the Father grants us our petition through St. Jude's prayers can vary, according to his perfect will. Let's take a look at a few ways it can happen:

A. Immediate relief. There are innumerable true stories which demonstrate St. Jude's power to bring speedy help. This one is taken from Mitch Finley's book:

Out of Gas on the Trans-Canada Highway

"Late night we – my uncle and aunt, my mother, a cousin, and myself – were out of gas on the Trans-Canada Highway," said Jeffrey D. of Dartmouth, Nova Scotia, "outside of St. John, New Brunswick. As usual, these things always happen at inconvenient times and places."

Jeffrey quickly sent "an SOS to God and my 'pal' Saint Jude." Within fifteen minutes, a tow truck arrived from an all-night garage. "My uncle flagged him down," Jeffrey said, "and he got us into St. John and the service station."

Right across from the garage was an elegant old hotel "in the grand Victorian style – the Admiral Beatty Hotel." Jeffrey's uncle explained to the hotel clerk about their predicament. "He put us up in the Royal Suite for the night at a nominal charge," Jeffrey said. "To say the least, I was flabbergasted at the spectacular answers to prayer on the part of Saint Jude."[10]

B. Got what we wanted after a wait. Persistence in prayer can educate us to be steadfast in faith. The prolonged wait for the fulfillment of our petition can be God's medicine for healing the infirmities of our souls, according to His will. This is arguably the greatest lesson I have personally learned from my devotion to St. Jude Thaddeus.

Jesus gives us the Parable of the Widow (Lk 18:1-8) to underscore the point that we "ought always to pray and not lose heart."

C. Didn't get what we wanted, but still got something good. We might not get exactly what we want, but St. Jude will benevolently guide us if we remain faithful. Robert Orsi tells of a woman who turned to St. Jude to cure her 15 year old son from the cancer he was diagnosed with. Despite her strong faith, her son died.

> Still, this woman did not feel that Jude had abandoned her. In time she played a role in opening a Ronald McDonald House for young cancer patients in her community, and she attributed her strength in this endeavor to the novenas she had been making to Jude since her son's cancer was discovered. The saint *had* heard her prayers, she was able to say bravely, but in a way she had not expected.[11]

D. Got what we wanted in a different way. On March 31, 2020, my period of active duty with the military was coming to an end on. I prayed to St. Jude Thaddeus to find a good job that would allow me to provide for my family.

My previous civilian work before this stint of duty was as an Explosive Detection K9 Handler. Keeping people in New York City safe by searching for bombs with my doggy partner was great work, but there was no going back to that company once my military orders ended. They were quite horrible and burned their bridges with me (as will be covered in (E) below).

So I reached out to some contacts, and within a short time had a new position with a great company all lined up. St. Jude came through.

Then the COVID-19 pandemic hit. The new company put a hiring freeze into effect exactly when I was about to join it, and when I needed it the most.

I never, ever, stopped praying to heaven for a resolution that would save my family from the impending crisis. And I did so confidently. I am not relating this to say that I pray any better than anyone else; it's just that it would be awfully cheeky of me to recommend living out the Gospel in a certain way but then not to do it myself.

March 31 came and went, and that was it. A new job search needed to begin to keep us afloat till things returned to normal. The following day, April 1, I spoke to a military contact who told me there were only a couple of spots open on a new mission to assist civil authorities in dealing with the novel coronavirus pandemic, and that they would be filled up that day.

I jumped on board faster than you could blink your eye. The mission continued for the rest of the year. I was not only able to bring my family back from the brink of disaster, but to do work that was valuable to my community, state, and country.

St. Jude really *really* came through, in ways I never could have foreseen.

E. Didn't get it yet, persistence in the face of an uncertain outcome. Until we know for certain the final outcome of a situation we are praying about, it is incumbent on us to continue praying.

Now, I mentioned above that I was a bomb dog handler. My K9's name is Mattie, and I had her from the time she was a young dog. I was her first and only handler. We worked with each other for five straight years, day and night, indoors and out, in heat and cold, in sun, rain, and snow. At work she was a professional, at home she was our family pet.

When Mattie was approaching retirement age, I went on military leave to serve my country in January of 2019. (This was the start of the active duty I mentioned above in (D)). Instead of allowing me to keep

Mattie during the time I was away, or retiring her in appreciation for her service and mine, and my family's sacrifice, the company took her away – permanently.

The company had no real financial or business incentive for doing this since they had hundreds of dogs and Mattie was at the end of her working days. The tearing away of Mattie from my family was the cruelest thing I ever personally experienced from a public entity.

My wife and I turned to St. Jude Thaddeus. Of course we did!

As of the date of this writing, two years have passed by and Mattie is not home yet. The company has not released her, and Mattie has been kept working at an undisclosed location, past when she should have been retired.

The fact is, we just do not know how our fight for justice will turn out in the end. However, we have received numerous indications which I believe are signs that St. Jude hears us.

When we went public with our struggle the reaction was intense. There was outrage against the company and overwhelming support for us. A lot of people got involved – social media, newspapers, television and radio from New York, New Jersey, and Ireland. State senators and congressmen wrote letters on our behalf.

We could not have predicted such intense and devoted support. Our change.org petition had nearly 250,000 signers by the start of 2021, and the numbers continue to rise.

While we have not yet achieved our ultimate goal of reuniting with Mattie, the movement we have built in the meantime is a testament to divine providence manifesting in a most benevolent manner. My gratitude knows no bounds; thank you, St. Jude!

(For more information on our struggle for Mattie, do an internet search for "BRING K9 MATTIE HOME").

Everybody Suffers

Every single person who is old enough to read this book has some kind of suffering in his or her life. This is a central and unavoidable component of human existence. But we are not to stand idly by – it's on us to figure out ways to mitigate suffering for ourselves and for others. By doing so we are following the divine commission to subdue the earth, to tame nature.

Suffering is also unequally distributed, and this is obvious. Some really decent people go through horrendous trials and some really bad people get away with literal murder. A Christian will trust that the Lord's providence will ensure that justice will always be done at the end of the day. He or she knows that the suffering we endure in the meantime is ultimately beneficial and benevolent.

At the Last Judgement, "we shall know the ultimate meaning of the whole work of creation and of the entire economy of salvation and understand the marvellous ways by which his Providence led everything towards its final end" (CCC 1040). This is simply **the most breathtaking thing** to look forward to, **the climax of the human adventure!**

Now here's a statement that some people will balk at: There is no value in a completely just distribution of suffering.

This might raise some eyebrows, but just imagine. Evil would always be immediately punished, good would always be immediately rewarded, and the chance to earn true merit in the eyes of God would be denied to us. There would be no chance for mercy, compassion, or proving ourselves worthy of Christ.

Please do not get me wrong – we should absolutely fight for justice in this life and should not take injustice lying down. I just want to bring you some comfort by bringing up that the divine justice system, so to speak, is infinitely better than anything anyone but God could come up with.

Poor in Spirit, Rich in Blessings

So **when** do Christians pray? In all circumstances, good or bad.

Praying in all circumstances shows heaven that our faith is real. As Christians who worship the true God and who are friends of His friend Jude Thaddeus, we pray through it all.

We pray in times of desperation, when the clouds of disaster loom.

We pray in times of elation, when we have been blessed with some kind of victory.

We pray in good times and in bad, in wealth or poverty, in sickness and in health, until through death we depart from this world to meet our eternal divine spouse.

Through all of it, through the entirety of our lives on earth, we recognize our own fragility and complete dependence on our Father who art in heaven. Jesus Christ is the vine, we are His branches, and without Him we can do nothing (Jn 15:5). The irony is that by lovingly accepting our total dependence, we become powerful beyond measure with the Almighty Lord's own power. "Blessed are the poor in spirit, for theirs is the kingdom of heaven" (Mt 5:3).

We should approach prayer with a certain balanced attitude. At one extreme, we should not be despondent – Christ our God flat out tells us, "Do not be anxious" (Mt 6:31-34). And furthermore, our hero St. Jude specializes in helping with this! At the other extreme, we should never be presumptuous or overconfident in our prayers. Presumption is a no-no (CCC 2092).

Those who pray in an authentic Christian manner are not naïve – they are fully aware of the dangers of life. And they can also feel two different things at the same time, as all humans can. We can be nervous or stressed about some situation we're dealing with and at the same time have an underlying serenity. This existential peace is a gift of the Holy Spirit that cannot be taken away, despite the dangers of life.

After all, how could we not be glowing with existential peace when we stand a good chance of living forever in perfect bliss, with anything we ever lost restored to us, and so much more on top of that?

This is the great hope of the Christian, and it is a hope that cannot be shaken because it is based on the Truth. We may be poor in spirit, but we are rich in blessings.

Let's place ourselves confidently into the hands of our all-loving heavenly Father and His Word and Son Jesus Christ. God is the lover of our souls.

It really is as simple as having faith in the gospel of Jesus Christ and living a life in accordance with that faith.

When Was St. Jude Around?

You might have gathered that since Jude Thaddeus is one of the Twelve Apostles of Jesus Christ, he walked on the earth in the first century A.D. You would be correct in that assertion.

Our entire calendar system is based on when Christ came to us in the flesh, with our years counting from when it was calculated that He was born. Thus, A.D. is from *Anno Domine* or "Year of the Lord." This rubs some non-Christian people the wrong way, so you will also see

C.E., representing "Common Era." But C.E. could also abbreviate "Christian Era" and in any case the years are counting forward from the same historical episode, the Nativity of our Lord.

So, St. Jude Thaddeus was there from the beginning of the catalytic events that led to the system of numbering years we still have today. It is unknown whether he was older or younger than Jesus. He would certainly have been roughly the same age, give or take a decade. As a family member, he would have had privileged knowledge of the Son of God as they both grew from boys into men.

Below is a timeline of some of the key events in the St. Jude devotion from that time till the early 21st century. All years are A.D. (obviously):

c. 40   Apostle Jude Thaddeus takes the burial shroud of our Lord and Savior Jesus Christ to the Aramaic-speaking city of Edessa. He uses the image of Christ on the shroud to cure Abgar, the city-state's king, of a hopeless case of leprosy. The city converts; Edessa becomes an early and influential outpost of Catholic Christianity.

c. 80   Towards the end of his life, the Apostle Jude writes an urgent letter to warn those under his care of the spiritual danger from certain false teachers. This epistle becomes a part of the New Testament of the Bible. Also, the liturgical prayer he used to celebrate the Eucharist evolves into the Anaphora of Addai (Thaddeus) and Mari, which is used to this day. Various traditions relate that he is martyred either in Armenia or Beirut, Lebanon. Disparate locations legitimately claim his tomb; his body was in fact divided for relics.

c. 90   Grandsons of the Apostle Jude are called before the Roman emperor Domitian to account for their Christianity and Davidic descent. They escape execution or imprisonment through their grandfather's heavenly intercession.

c. 200   St. Clement of Alexandria mentions Thaddeus in connection with Edessa, reporting that his remains were buried in the royal cemetery.[12]

301   Official adoption by Armenia of Christianity as the national religion. It is the first country in the world to do so. Jude Thaddeus was the first to bring the Gospel to Armenia, along with the Apostle Bartholomew.

525   Burial shroud of the Lord, lost for four and a half centuries, is rediscovered during the restoration of Edessa's city wall following a flood. It was hidden in a part of the wall above a gate which had the inscription (likely in Aramaic), "O Christ our God, no one who hopes in you will ever be put to shame."

944   The holy burial shroud, now known as the Mandylion, is rescued from Saracen (Muslim)-occupied Edessa by a Greek army under General John Kourkouas. It is then transported in triumph to the holy imperial city of Constantinople.

1153   St. Bernard of Clairvaux expresses a great devotion to St. Jude, who he credits with preserving his chastity, and is buried with a relic of the Apostle.

1204   The Mandylion, the burial shroud of Jesus Christ, is stolen from Constantinople by mostly French "Crusaders."

1353   The Mandylion publicly reemerges in the possession of the French knight Geoffrey de Charny. Around the same time, Jesus Christ speaks to St. Birgitta of Sweden (1303-73) about St. Jude Thaddeus, telling her to turn to him in confidence.

1531   The Mother of God appears to St. Cuauhtlatoatzin in Mexico City and leaves an image not made by human hands on his cloak. Mary is to be known in this context as Our Lady of Guadalupe. Centuries later, in Chicago, a parish dedicated to Our Lady of Guadalupe hosts the St. Jude shrine that catapults the Apostle to unprecedented international attention.

1548   Pope Paul III grants a plenary indulgence to all who would visit the tomb of St. Jude in Rome on his Latin rite feast of October 28. (Relics of his are buried in Rome, he was not martyred there). A plenary indulgence is a complete remission of punishment for sins that have been forgiven. In other words, once your sins are forgiven, indulgences save you from having to make a more painful restitution to God. They save you time in Purgatory!

1578   The burial shroud of Christ is brought from France to Turin in Italy, where it has remained to this day. The Mandylion – first safeguarded and transported by Jude Thaddeus, is now usually known as the Holy Shroud of Turin.

1702   Creation of a Spanish language novena to St. Jude, a copy of which is now held in the Sutro Library in California.

1826   Publication in Latin of a booklet called the *Officium Parvum*, the Little Office of St. Jude, in which the Apostle is acknowledged as "the special advocate of the unfortunate and well-nigh hopeless."

1911   The Claretian Missionary Fathers build a shrine to St. Jude in Santiago, Chile. His devotion is promoted among prostitutes and others on the fringes of society.

1916   The Pallottines start the St. Jude Shrine in Baltimore, Maryland, the oldest one in the United States.

1929   The Claretians start the National Shrine of St. Jude at Our Lady of Guadalupe Church in Chicago, Illinois. The Dominican Shrine of St. Jude Thaddeus opens the same year in the same city. The devotion gains great national popularity.

1962   Opening of St. Jude Children's Research Hospital in Memphis, Tennessee. It was founded by entertainer Danny Thomas in thanksgiving to Jude Thaddeus for his timely and decisive intercession in his life. The St. Jude devotion has a tremendous worldwide popularity by this time.

2021   *HEAVEN HELP US, NOW! A Self Help Guide to God's Own First Responder, St. Jude Thaddeus* is published.

A dramatic shift in the St. Jude devotion took place in the 1960's. Just when it had achieved a certain peak of prestige, devotion to saints and traditional popular piety in general came under attack within the Church. Some proposed reforms were valid, such as the need to eliminate the intrusion of superstition into devotionalism.

But for the most part, the shift away from popular piety was driven by faithless or misguided clergy and ignorant or apathetic laity. The Church was not immune to the general decline in societal values suffered by the West. I firmly believe that behind it all was a large-scale demonic assault on the Church, one which is ongoing. The machinations of evil preternatural forces in human affairs is as real as you and I are.

A great book I recommend on this topic is *The Devil in the City of Angels* by Jesse Romero. The author is a faithful Catholic and a veteran of the Los Angeles County Sheriff's Department. He draws on his personal experiences with the demonic to bring a timely Christian message to our world.

As it turns out, St. Jude Thaddeus is a powerful warrior against Satan, according to God Himself! Jesus told St. Birgitta of Sweden that he had "purity of heart and bravely fought the devil."[13] Perhaps this has something to do with the resilience of his popularity.

Despite the overall damage inflicted on Catholic devotionalism, St. Jude's followers were sufficiently numerous and loyal for the devotion to him to continue on with comparative strength for the rest of the 20th century. For instance, the book *Thank You, St. Jude* by Robert A. Orsi, published in 1996, noted that the Claretian Shrine of St. Jude in Chicago was getting about *three thousand* pieces of mail *a day* from Jude's followers.

However, there is no doubt that many, many more people could benefit from Jude's help but don't even know who he is. *Heaven Help*

Us, Now! has been written to help correct this situation. Let's help suffering souls and spread the word about God's own first responder!

6

Why

Why on earth would someone take the crazy step of speaking to a person who can't be seen? What is in it for us to make this leap of faith?

POWER. Infinite power.

That may not sound like the most religious way of saying it, but please do hear me out.

Sometime in the late 20th century, there was this American late night TV show called *Politically Incorrect*, hosted by a guy called Bill Maher. I found it entertaining, even though I disagreed with the host about two-thirds of the time. Well, one time he had a guest (I forget the name, it doesn't matter) who asserted that religious faith was for mentally weak people to feel empowered, and Maher agreed.

OOH BOY did they both have it wrong!

These people who think they're strong without God are kidding themselves. Human existence is inherently fragile in every way – physically, mentally, emotionally, spiritually. Our success as a species in fulfilling the divine commission to fill the earth and subdue it (Gn 1:28) seems to have left many of us with our noses in the air. Indeed, the Lord's mercy in allowing us to achieve such stunning success has ironically led many to reject God, or at least to be slothful in regard to the divine.

Much of the world – in fact, the entire developed world – has electricity, the internet, literacy, plentiful food and water, knowledge of science and medicine, complex civilizations, cars, trains, planes, and the list goes on and on. Compare the early 21st century with the tough times of the Stone Age, and you can easily see how far we have come.

And yet, instead of glorifying God and rejoicing in the Gospel, the world is saturated with news about terrorism, pandemics, and tyrannical governments. Essentially, humanity has collectively abused God's mercy. Our kind has elevated itself to a position of false divinity, just like at the Tower of Babel (Gn 11:1-9).

There is a cure for this, and it's called "the gospel of Jesus Christ, the Son of God" (Mk 1:1). He through whom "all things were made" (Jn 1:3) actually "became flesh and dwelt among us" (Jn 1:14) in order to give us His Gospel. We humans are so astoundingly blessed to have the Creator of reality, Reality Himself, explain reality to us.

Let's keep in mind His criticism of lukewarm people – Jesus did not mince words in letting them know how much He detests their mindset: "For you say, I am rich, I have prospered, and I need nothing; not knowing that you are wretched, pitiable, poor, blind, and naked" (Rv 3:17). But if we lovingly embrace the notion that we are truly poor no matter what our earthly possessions or position, it's then that God makes us rich. In fact, this is the first Beatitude the Lord gives us: "Blessed are the poor in spirit, for theirs is the kingdom of heaven" (Mt 5:3).

Eat Some Humble Pie

To call on St. Jude effectively, we need to eat a slice of humble pie. Having the correct internal disposition is a necessary means to an end, but it's also an end in its own right. Humility might be an acquired taste, but it's really quite healthy!

Here are the major nutritional benefits:

1. It allows us to know our true place, to accept the truth of our weakness in the universe and our complete dependence on God.

2. It allows us to access and experience the omnipotence that only God has, and which He shares with us through His chosen servants, such as St. Jude Thaddeus.

Gaining this wisdom is a major reason **why** we should call upon St. Jude, and do everything on our end to make our praying effective. We are just better off in every way through devotion to St. Jude. Not only do we have the joy of having an immediate and tangible need taken care of, but we become truly strong people on a deep level. We become durable, resilient, and empowered.

This is true strength, not the fragile puffery of those who rely only on themselves. Like branches that are cut from a tree, worldly people might be under the illusion that they are strong until they dry up, wither, and die because they're cut off from their source of life.

Quite in contradiction to the mocking of scoffers, popular Catholic devotions, properly practiced, are an emblem of strength and liveliness. In particular, St. Jude's faithful followers are not a bunch known for dour pouting. They have a fortitude which allows them to sustain humor in tough times. They are able to bring joyful fun to living life because their peace comes from heaven.

As the scholar Robert Orsi aptly put it, "The discipline of praying to Jude was not the harsh stoicism endorsed in devotional culture, however, but a courageous response to life's troubles undertaken with love and trust."[14]

The Divine Toolkit

A facet of human existence that distinguishes us from the rest of the Animal Kingdom is our use of tools. Even those species which have some rudimentary tool use, such as chimpanzees, are dwarfed by man's abilities in this regard. No other natural creature comes close.

This is one of the ways in which humans are in the likeness of God, in that He similarly works through His creatures. We humans work with tools out of necessity, in order to extend the limited capabilities of our bodies and minds; the Lord does so because He loves everything He created.

I wish to underscore this point. When Jesus was being arrested He said, "Do you think that I cannot appeal to my Father, and He will at once send me more than twelve legions of angels?" (Mt 26:53). He expressed a similar sentiment only a few hours later when He was being interviewed by the Roman prefect Pontius Pilate. He told Pilate, "My kingship is not of this world; if my kingship was of this world, my servants would fight" (Jn 18:36).

The bigger point, of course, is that Christ voluntarily gave Himself over to be executed by crucifixion in order to save mankind. According to the rules of existence which He Himself devised, this was the necessary price to pay to make possible our freedom from the clutches of Satan.

But we might notice something else in the hypothetical scenario Christ brought up. If He was going to extricate Himself from that situation, why would He rely on His servants to fight for Him? Why would He have His Father send Him angels instead of simply willing Himself out of it?

Because God delights in His creation. He loves when what He created fulfills what He created it to do. Otherwise, what is the point of anything besides God existing?

In the beginning, God saw what He brought into existence, "and God saw that it was good" (Gn 1:9). He lets creation do its thing – the natural universe, the extra-natural universe, and everything in them. "For you love all things that exist, / and you loathe none of the things which you have made, / for you would not have made anything if you had hated it" (Wis 11:24).

What About Evil?

But hey, what about evil? If God loves everything, doesn't that mean He loves evil too?

Ah hah! I never thought you'd ask.

Evil is the rejection of God. He loves the free will He gave us, but not the evil that results from our abuse of it. "Those who dwelt of old in your holy land / you hated for their detestable practices, / their works of sorcery and unholy rites, / their merciless slaughter of children" (Wis 12:3-5). By the way, notice that among the "detestable practices" that provoke the Lord's hatred is the "merciless slaughter of children." Abortion supporters beware – God also loves His perfect justice, and it is severe.

Thankfully, "all sins will be forgiven the sons of men" (Mk 3:28) if we "repent, and believe in the gospel" (Mk 1:15), so it's in our best interest to run to His mercy while there is still time.

You Are The General Of Your War

We are at war. Our spiritual battles are every bit as real as armed conflict between human parties. I am saying this as a combat veteran – the *true* war is the one against the evil one. It is every bit as violent and requires the same vigilance to soldier skills, tactics, and strategy. As the Church teaches us:

> "This dramatic situation of 'the whole world [which] is in the power of the evil one' makes man's life a battle: The whole of man's history has been the story of dour combat with the powers of evil, stretching, so our Lord tells us, from the very dawn of history until the last day" (CCC 409).

The war rages on the level of both individual souls as well as larger societies. We will eventually see and fully understand this reality when we pass into the eternal, "for there is nothing hidden, except to be made manifest; nor is anything secret, except to come to light" (Mk 4:22).

So, **why** is it beneficial to call upon St. Jude for our personal trials? I will speak from my military knowledge. Generals such as Patton, Washington, or Napoléon get the credit for victories in battle and in war. Yet, they rarely if ever do any close quarter combat themselves. What general officers actually do is marshal resources and concentrate forces to achieve victory.

The classic work *Small Unit Leadership: A Commonsense Approach* by "Ranger" Mike Malone explains that generals, "must bring about a winning combination of forces" and "make support systems work." They "bring together units, fire support, and supplies at the right place and time for battle."[15]

This is where Jude Thaddeus the Apostle comes in. As God's own first responder, He is a powerful resource in the Lord's arsenal. Jesus Christ gives him to us so that we can have him as a powerful resource in our own lives, which in turn leads us to Christ and eternal life.

Why Jesus Gave Us Jude

It is clear that our Lord wants us to be truly happy. He does want us to take the initiative to *do* things to achieve joy, including the action of praying, of *asking* Him.

As He said to His disciples during the Last Supper, "Truly, truly, I say to you, if you ask anything of the Father, he will give it to you in my name. Until now you have asked nothing in my name; ask, and you will receive, *that your joy may be complete* [emphasis added]" (Jn 16:23-24).

Christ could not be more emphatic: "Whatever you ask in my name, I will do it, that the Father may be glorified in the Son; if you ask anything in my name, I will do it" (Jn 14:13-14).

Interestingly though, what He said right before this was, "Truly, truly, I say to you, he who believes in me will also do the works that I do; and *greater works than these will he do* [emphasis added], because I go to the Father" (Jn 14:12).

Wait, what's this – is Jesus saying that there will be people greater than Him?

No way. Of course not.

He is saying that He will be with His Father in heaven and thus physically invisible to mankind on earth. However, He will be made manifest through the work of His servants. Almost the entirety of miracles that have ever been recorded happened *after* the Ascension of Christ to His Father. But in every case, it is always the saving power of the Lord at work, even if He cannot be seen. The signs and wonders He works through His servants are for our benefit, to help lead us to salvation.

It is clear that Christ wants us to access His power.

The miracles Christ did during His earthly ministry were incidental to His main mission of being the Paschal sacrifice for our sins. Yet, they were driven by His merciful compassion for people's individual circumstances. They were also signs that hinted at His true identity. The miracles He allows us in our own day and age through St. Jude's prayers serve the same function, giving people relief in pressing situations and also leading them to the true faith and salvation.

Remember, Jesus loves to work through His creatures and is enthusiastic about dispensing aid through His chosen intermediaries. This is **why** He gave us St. Jude Thaddeus!

Those who are close to Jude are truly fortunate, because they have a particularly intimate path of access to the Almighty.

Job: Precursor of Jude

The story of Job clearly illustrates that it is in our best interest to approach God through the intermediaries he has appointed to us.

Do you remember Job? He is the protagonist of the Book of Job which typically appears just before the Book of Psalms in the Old Testament of the Bible. His patience was proverbial. Saying that someone who is capable of putting up with a lot has "the patience of Job" bears witness to the influence of his story.

Job was a pious and prosperous chieftain who was suddenly hit with a number of calamities, the most heartbreaking of which was the death of all ten of his children. He was then struck with a rather severe dermatological affliction – boils covered his body from head to toe.

Some of Job's friends came by to express sympathy for him in his distress. But they also insisted that he must have committed some grave sin for God to punish him with such severe suffering. In this, they were completely wrong.

While St. Jude was certainly patient, and he suffered in his life (he was martyred, after all), it was a different detail of Job's story that serves as a precursory example for **why** we should turn to Jude Thaddeus.

The Book of Job touches on numerous profound topics, such as the influence of Satan in human affairs, the suffering of the innocent, and the need to trust God's merciful providence. For our purposes here, the big lesson comes at the very end.

Through Job's intense trials, he ended up even more trusting of God than ever before, greatly pleasing the Lord with his humble fidelity. On the other hand, God was angry at the "friends" for falsely imputing guilt to His servant Job. The Lord speaks to one of them:

My wrath is kindled against you and against your two friends ... go to my servant Job, and offer up for yourselves a burnt offering; and my servant Job shall pray for you, for *I will accept His prayer* [emphasis added] not to deal with you according to your folly (Jb 42:7-8).

God clearly wanted to forgive the friends or He would not have told them how to gain forgiveness. But He tells them to go through Job! He tells them to go through an intermediary of proven holiness in order to have their petition granted.

It works the same way with St. Jude Thaddeus, and this is a major reason **why** we should call upon him in desperate difficulties, hopeless cases, impossible situations, and lost causes.

We can hear God say, "Go to my servant Jude Thaddeus, and he shall pray for you, for I will accept his prayer!"

Why Does St. Jude Help Us?

Why does St. Jude do what he does? Let us take another look at his second name: **Thaddeus**. As we saw in Chapter 2, this name expresses the distinguishing traits of his character. Jesus explained to St. Birgitta that it means "amiable" and "loving";[16] it also means "magnanimous," according to Pope Benedict XVI.[17] You get the picture.

Jude Thaddeus himself had received so much goodness from the Lord in his lifetime; he was one of the fortunate ones, "privileged" if you will, by the grace of God. He was not content to keep it to himself. He *had* to selflessly share the Gospel, even if it meant his martyrdom. His sympathetic heart compels him to continue helping us in the present day, many centuries after he went to his Maker.

We can feel his concern for the plight of mankind in his only recorded spoken line in the Bible. The Gospel of John (14:22) describes him at the Last Supper: "Judas (not Iscariot) said to him, 'Lord, how is it that you will manifest yourself to us, and not to the world?'" We can detect in Jude's question a sense of unworthiness at being so blessed, and a desire that the Lord would spread the Good News to everyone.

Jesus answered him, "If a man loves me, he will keep my word, and my Father will love him, and we will come to him and make our home with him. He who does not love me does not keep my words; and the word which you hear is not mine but the Father's who sent me. These things I have spoken to you, while I am still with you. But the Counselor, the Holy Spirit whom the Father will send in my name, he will teach you all things and bring to your remembrance all that I have said to you. (Jn 14:23-26).

Christ's reply to Jude might not seem like an obvious answer to his question, but it is a profound one. He is telling Jude that what somebody has to do for the Lord Jesus to manifest to them is to love Jesus and keep His word. For people to come to love Jesus Christ in the first place, it was up to Jude and his fellow Apostles to go forth with the Holy Spirit that the Father was sending them. Our Lord Jesus Christ was to manifest to the world through servants of His who were to be filled with His Spirit!

It was evidently significant enough of an interaction for St. John the Theologian to remember and record it, under the inspiration of the Holy Spirit.

This explains the fervor with which Jude Thaddeus preached the true faith in life, and **why** he continues his perpetual apostolate for *us* from heaven. Once he understood that it was up to him to manifest Christ to the world, he made it his life's mission to do so. It was not up to him alone, of course, but to all the Apostles and every disciple of the

Lord. But he did everything that *he* could do. The diverse qualities of his unique God-given personality were put in service to the Gospel.

Jude Thaddeus is a fighter, a warrior.

Through his prayers on our behalf in the presence of God Himself, Jude the Apostle wishes to bring to us the joyous exultation that a soul feels when Christ is manifested. This is the exact same joyous exultation expressed by the holy man Simeon in the temple of Jerusalem. Over two thousand years ago, St. Simeon knew he would see the promised Messiah because the Holy Spirit had revealed it to him. There was no scientific evidence that explained it to him; he just *knew* because his faith was real.

And when the baby Jesus came to the temple 40 days after his birth, "according to the custom of the Law," the moment had come for Simeon:

...who took him up in his arms and blessed God and said,

"Lord, now let your servant depart in peace, according to your word;

for my eyes have seen your salvation

which you have prepared in the presence of all peoples,

a light for revelation to the Gentiles, and for glory to your people Israel" (Lk 2:27-32).

Christ, even as a baby, manifested His Gospel to Simeon through His Holy Spirit.

It is this same Gospel of Christ that manifests to us when we are rescued from a hopeless situation through the prayers of St. Jude. This is exactly what Jude wants for us and **why** he does what he does. May the intercession of St. Jude Thaddeus the Apostle allow us to experience the joy of Simeon!

CHAPTER

7

How

This chapter does not deal with the how-to of calling on St. Jude, but rather with **how it works**. That is, by what mechanism does something so lacking in physical substance as prayer cause reality itself to shift in our favor?

In a way, it seems pretty outlandish to claim that by turning your heart, mind, and words in a certain manner, you can change what happens in the world. Somehow, a scenario envisioned in your head becomes real. The wooden puppet Pinocchio really becomes a human boy. *Come on man, who are you kidding.*

Intuitively, we humans sense that we are weak. Don't get me wrong, there is a lot of talk about people claiming to be strong. But look at normal human behavior – a healthy fear keeps most people from walking too close to the edge of a cliff. We all know we would go *splat* if we fell down a thousand foot precipice.

But yet, we can cause x, y, and z to happen simply by praying for it? **How** is this possible?

What is "God"?

Let's take things back to the beginning, the very beginning. Before the beginning of time and space...

Hold on, we cannot accurately say "before" the beginning because such a term would indicate the presence of time. Alas, there is no real way around using terminology founded upon temporal notions because eternity is not an experience to which our brains can relate. The result is that we have to explicate the infinite within the confines of our finite descriptive capabilities, because that's all we got.

So, "before" the beginning of time and space, what was there? What does existence consist of in its essence? Well, that "ultimate reality" *is* infinite power, infinite wisdom, infinite love. It is *alive*. It is that Supreme Being who in the English language we know as "God."

Out of His selfless love God created the universe. He created us humans in His own image and likeness. And He definitively revealed His true nature to mankind when He told Moses His name, "I am who am" (Ex 3:14). God simply *IS*.

The Lord Saves

God's revelation of His existence and nature was part of His plan of salvation for us. Way back in prehistoric times, the Lord God breathed a soul into the man we call Adam, and thus the human race as we know it came into existence. God created and ensouled a wife for Adam shortly after. But Adam and his wife Eve fell into sin, the "Original Sin." Since they are the progenitors of our species, this corruption of human nature was passed along in our spiritual DNA, so to speak.

But the Lord had a plan to rescue us. He, God the eternal Word, whom "all things were made through" (Jn 1:3) came to us in the flesh. Like, literally. This was a historical event that occurred in the land of Israel some two millennia before this book you are reading was pub-lished. God became a human being. And He stayed God at the same time.

I am speaking of "my Lord and my God" (Jn 20:28), Jesus Christ. He chose his own name *Jesus*, which means "the Lord saves," and which succinctly expressed the purpose of His mission among us. He not only came to us in the flesh but offered Himself, in the flesh, as a bloody sacrifice to His Father for the salvation of mankind. Then, He rose Himself from the dead. Physically, literally. The Resurrection was a historical event.

He paved the way for all of us. Since no servant is greater than his master, and He died, we will also die. But now the door is open to us to *choose* to believe and be saved. This is an option that was not available to humanity previous to our Lord's execution and Resurrection. Those who lived before the gates of heaven were opened and who were holy were saved in anticipation of the sacrifice to come. But their souls had to wait until Christ was crucified to get into heaven.

You Better Believe It!

As for us, how do we know that we have to believe to be saved? Because Jesus Christ tells us. After His Resurrection He specifically told Jude Thaddeus and the other Apostles, "Go into all the world and preach the gospel to the whole creation. He who believes and is baptized will be saved; but he who does not believe will be condemned" (Mk 16:15-16). There you have it.

And so *belief, faith* is **how** it all works. It is necessary not only for our eternal salvation, but for the granting of petitions having to do with our life on Earth. It is the mechanism by which we access the infinite power of God.

Faith In Action

The Gospels show clearly how this actually works in practice. Early in His ministry, Jesus preached in the synagogue in his hometown of Nazareth. "Many who heard him were astonished ... And they took offense at him" (Mk 6:2-3). The townspeople's personal familiarity with Jesus and his family led them to disparage Him; familiarity breeds contempt, as the saying goes. Ironically, one of the relatives of the Lord who was known and named by the townspeople as an excuse for their unbelief was St. Jude (Judas): "Is not this the carpenter, the son of Mary and brother of James and Joses and Judas and Simon, and are not his sisters here with us?" (Mk 6:3a).

As a result of this hostility, "*he could do no mighty work there* [emphasis added], except that he laid his hands upon a few sick people and healed them. And he marveled because of their *unbelief* [emphasis added]" (Mk 6:5-6).

Of course, Christ certainly could have worked a miracle in absolute terms. But it is clear from scripture that the Lord set up a certain supernatural law regarding the answer to prayer that is as certain as any law of physics or mathematics. This is the law: one must have faith in the Lord for Him to grant a petition, for Him to do a mighty work beyond His regularly perceivable awesomeness. He has granted the power to change the course of history to us mere mortals, a power that is only accessible through faith in Him.

Please bear in mind that God already does awesome things that people tend to take for granted because our appreciation is dulled by our fallen state. You know, little things like creating everything that exists and establishing the laws of the universe.

And the Lord will certainly intervene in a miraculous way when He sees fits, with or without our belief. For instance, St. Paul was at first a hateful persecutor of the Church, but one day Christ appeared to him in a vision without any prior warning. Incidentally, he was instantly converted.

However, in ordinary circumstances **faith** is the necessary precondition for God to share His power with us. For a definition of faith, there is not one better than the one given in the Bible in the Letter to the Hebrews: "Now faith is the assurance of things hoped for, the conviction of things not seen" (11:1). If we are being judged on whether or not we have faith, and we are only judged by what we do with our free will, the logical conclusion is that faith is a choice.

Faith also happens to be a supernatural gift of the Holy Spirit, given to us by the Father. But the first step to getting it is to agree to believe. Just crack the door of your heart open!

Be Like a Child

A certain humility, a child-like trust, is required for this acceptance of "things not seen." Jesus explicitly tells us this. "Truly, I say to you, whoever does not receive the kingdom of God like a child shall not enter it" (Lk 18:17). A heart that has been hardened by the trauma of life might find this difficult. But the more we open up to God and His saints the more they will rush in and restore our innocence. This opens us up even more to the Lord, who will in turn infuse us with His grace to a correspondingly greater degree. God will always outpace us; this is exactly the kind of snowball effect we want!

On the other side of the aisle are those who do not believe or do not trust – those who lack faith. Among these are people who openly mock the piety of the faithful. Even among intellectually arrogant Catholics there are those who belittle traditional popular devotions. Well, neither the Gospel at large nor the St. Jude devotion in particular has room for scoffers.

Those who are wise in their own eyes and look down on the trusting clients of Jude Thaddeus do so at their own peril. It is Christ Himself who delights in keeping pretentious unbelievers in the dark: "At that time Jesus declared, 'I thank you, Father, Lord of heaven and earth, that you have hidden these things from the wise and understanding and revealed them to infants; yes, Father, for such was your gracious will'" (Mt 11:25-26).

By the way, please do not wrongly interpret our Lord and think He's telling us to be ignorant in life. Quite the contrary. We are to be like infants in terms of our innocence – our complete trust in God and our experiential ignorance of evil (It's really not cool to be one of the bad kids who think they're cool). By softening our hearts in such a manner, we are actually opening ourselves up to being wiser and more understanding than those considered by the world to be so. It's a desirable thing to have such innocence in regard to the things of God while simultaneously being learned in the arts and sciences the world has to offer. "Brethren, do not be children in your thinking; be infants in evil, but in thinking be mature" (1 Cor 14:20).

A truly faithful Christian is called to have a well-rounded intellect, enlightened by divine wisdom, secular knowledge, and practical sense. It all goes to understanding the Truth, a.k.a. Jesus Christ. If you keep this in mind, you will stand to gain the maximum possible benefit from being a devotee of St. Jude Thaddeus.

How is it that St. Jude has this particular power?

We will now examine **how** it is that Jude Thaddeus, of all people, has the power to help people who turn to him in desperation.

The positive traits of a soul's personality stay with it forever if it makes it to heaven. As we have seen, Thaddeus means "amiable, loving," and this was an appellation he received during his earthly life for qualities that he embodied. These distinguishing qualities are now magnified beyond description and they are his to keep, forever.

In essence, our lives in this universe are a proving ground for what we will be doing in the next life. Jesus tells us a parable about a man who went on a journey and left his money under the care of three servants (Mt 25:14-30). This represents Jesus leaving the care of His Church to us on Earth until He returns in glory.

When the man returned from his trip, he settled the accounts with the servants under whose care he left his money. This represents us meeting Christ our Judge at the end of our life or at His Second Coming, whichever comes first. To those servants who were able to make a profit for their master in his absence with the money entrusted to them, greater responsibility and honor was given. The man said to each of them, "Well done, good and faithful servant; you have been faithful over a little, I will set you over much; enter into the joy of your master."

The end goal of our lives on Earth is to have Jesus say this to us!

These words of Christ hold the key to understanding St. Jude's power. Notice that the work done by the good servants in their master's absence is considered to be "a little." It is only when they enter the joy of their master, in heaven, that they are "set ... over much."

The Lord was confirming in His earthly ministry what He had already revealed in the Old Testament. This is what the Book of Wisdom has to say: "But the souls of the righteous are in the hand of God, / and no torment will ever touch them. / In the eyes of the foolish they seemed to have died, ... but they are at peace" (3:1-3). Okay, that much most Christians already accept as part of the faith. The faithful departed are or will be in eternal peace with God. But wait, get this: "They will govern nations and rule over peoples, / and the Lord will reign over them for ever" (3:8). This is an astounding revelation. Basically, the righteous are granted eternal rulership over particular domains.

The Church elucidates this idea further. Concerning the saints, the *Catechism* (2683) tells us that, "when they entered the joy of their Master, they were 'put in charge of many things.' Their intercession is their most exalted service to God's plan." They're here to help (well, they're in heaven but you know what I mean), and their intercession is amplified when we participate in this salvific work by calling upon them. This is why "we can and should ask them to intercede for us and the whole world."

In the case of Jude Thaddeus, it is apparent that one of the domains in the temporal sphere over which he has dominion is that of rescuing people from the most desperate, hopeless situations. As such, it would truly behoove us to take full advantage of his freely given and empowering help. He will strengthen us to overcome our greatest challenges and take care of things beyond our control or ken.

St. Jude's supernatural power was born from an overflow of God's completely gratuitous mercy. This is how it works, and now, **how** we ask him to use this power is entirely in our hands.

8

Prayers To St. Jude Thaddeus

This chapter contains a treasury of wonderful prayers to St. Jude Thaddeus. None of these rule out spontaneously talking to him; in fact, such spontaneity is to be encouraged. But as I brought up earlier, these prayers were composed to help us focus our thoughts while communicating with heaven. They have been made holy, sanctified by many decades (and sometimes centuries) of faithful devotees of God's own "first responder." Innumerable thousands of people have benefitted from the help of St. Jude gained through these prayers.

I have selected the prayers included here from a variety of authoritative sources. The first three are from the Melkite Catholic Church's *Publican's Prayer Book*, and from the Byzantine Catholic Church's *Menaion*; the rest are from works in the public domain. Often, several versions of the same prayer are in circulation. I have harmonized them for consistency in usage, punctuation, and mechanics.

These prayers do not constitute an exhaustive compilation – you can easily find others out there. But I have attempted to provide a selection that covers the major areas that Jude Thaddeus specializes in. There is a great spiritual wealth contained in them; calling the collection a 'treasury' is truly appropriate.

These prayers should be said in conjunction with others sanctified by Christian tradition, pride of place in popular devotion going to the Blessed Mother's Holy Rosary. We also have the Jesus Prayer and the Divine Mercy Chaplet, among others.

As we move on to the solid food of our life of prayer, we draw closer to the Liturgy. To help us along the way, the first three prayers here are, in fact, liturgical. We can go further and take part in the public prayer of the Church, known as the Divine Office or the Liturgy of the Hours. Then, as we climb the mountain towards God we approach the Sacraments. And the peak of this mountain, both the summit and source of all our blessings, is our Lord Jesus Christ Himself in the Eucharist. He comes to us in the literal flesh during the Divine Liturgy, the Mass. Jesus Christ is the ultimate "solid food" of our faith, literally. He is the source of St. Jude's power to help us in our distress.

So let's take a read through all this richness.

1. Kontakion of St. Jude

O Apostle Jude, Brother of the Lord and His witness,
A preacher of Christ perfect in your wisdom,
You come forth from a noble ancestry.
You nourished the whole world with the wealth of your doctrine,
Teaching the Orthodox Faith of the Lord,
For you are closely related to Christ, the Source of Grace.

This is the Byzantine Kontakion for the feast of the Apostle Jude on June 19. A kontakion is a short poetic sermon which teaches about the saint or topic in question. In liturgical use, it is chanted after the opening antiphons during the Divine Liturgy. It is short enough to easily remember, and given its teaching purpose and lyrical qualities, I encourage you to do so.

Remember, when we say 'Orthodox' here, we are not necessarily talking about the churches of our brethren who use that title but who are not in communion with the Rock of Rome, the Pope. We say it to mean *correct belief.*

There is a great book by the legendary Catholic writer G.K. Chesterton titled, "Orthodoxy"; I highly recommend it.

2. Troparion of St. Jude (June 19 Feast Day)

O Holy Jude, we offer you a hymn of praise, seeing that you are a kinsman of the Lord, a courageous martyr triumphant over error, and a keeper of the Faith. Wherefore, celebrating your holy memory today, we obtain by your prayers the remission of our sins.

This is the Byzantine Troparion for the feast day of St. Jude. A Troparion is a short hymn which intends to epitomize the very essence of the celebration. Like the Kontakion, it is of ancient origin, dating back to the first millennium of Christianity. In the Divine Liturgy it is chanted right before the Kontakion, so that the Troparion and Kontakion are in essence back-to-back and can present the appearance of being a single hymn.

Even though they are said liturgically on a particular day of the year, we can pray the Troparion and Kontakion in our private devotions on any day, just take out (the) references to "today," etc.

And if you do so, I say again that it is more effective to combine our prayers to St. Jude with other holy prayers: the Lord's Prayer (Our Father), the Angelic Salutation (Hail Mary), and the Jesus Prayer. And then there is the Chaplet of Divine Mercy, and the Rosary, which are longer devotions that use many of the basic prayers as building blocks. To help anyone who wants to learn how to pray these devotions properly, I have appended guidance at the end of this book.

3. Troparion of the Apostle Thaddeus
(August 21 Feast Day)

An eye-witness of the God who appeared to you in body, O Apostle Thaddeus, as His holy disciple you shone the grace of the Savior upon those in darkness. The people of Edessa came to see a wondrous healer in you; now protect all those who run to you in faith.

Edessa rejoiced today at its baptism through you. Abgar has been freed from passion and praises you. We join in his hymn, and we sing to you: Fill our lives with spiritual happiness and heal our passion by your prayers, O Apostle Thaddeus.

This Troparion is for the feast day of our special saint under his second name Thaddeus. In this case, his apostleship to the people of Edessa is highlighted. We can see the connection between Thaddeus' courageous and compassionate heart and the seeds of devotion to him as the saint of the desperate and hopeless. It was in Edessa that he first came to prominence as "a wonderous healer." It was he who transported to Edessa the relic of the greatest miracle of all time, the Resurrection of the Messiah. And now, he has the power through Christ to protect all of us who run to him *with faith*.

The second paragraph of the prayer is actually the Byzantine Ruthenian version of the Troparion, and it made it into this book at the last minute. Here's the story.

I used to smoke cigarettes. I ended that habit some years back but switched to chewing tobacco. Now it was getting to the point that I wanted to stop that too, but I was hopelessly addicted. My plan was to attempt quitting in the upcoming year, like for Lent or something.

It seems that Jude Thaddeus had some other plans for me. On the eve of the feast of the Apostle Thaddeus the year in which I wrote this (2020), I was stricken with some of the most intense pain I have ever felt. It first hit me right after I had a nice thick wad of dip (chewing tobacco) in my lip. It felt as if someone smashed me in the teeth with a hammer. The torturous sensation seared right through my teeth, gums, and into my jaw.

I took it as a sign, especially since I was writing a book on the saint of hopeless causes and was well aware of the date. The pain did not go away the next day, the feast itself.

That's it, I'm done. No more tobacco. Kick the habit. Thaddeus will help. And the pain? Get some real value out of it – offer it to our Father in heaven in reparation for all my sins.

I was off from work that day and we had a Divine Liturgy (Mass) at my parish. Needless to say, I was rather ecstatic that we were having the Eucharistic celebration on this special feast. I typically cantor on the weekdays if I am off from work so I had to familiarize myself with the Troparion. As I read it, my eyes opened wide. Here was Thaddeus doing the impossible and freeing Abgar from passion – that is, freeing him from a disordered desire or addiction.

I was like, wow, another sign from heaven. Pretty cool. If there was any doubt in my mind about the direction I was going to take, or about the spiritual significance of the timing, this settled it.

I was thankful to God for allowing me a once-in-a-lifetime chance to make my body a living sacrifice (Rom 12:1) through giving up my reliance on nicotine. I very consciously united my tiny suffering with the incomparable suffering of Christ on the Cross, as a member of His Body. This made it abundantly worthwhile; I knew I was helping to pay for my sins and those of my loved ones. In a word, it was penance.

And I have not gone back to the bad habit, an addiction really. Oh, it was tough at times, but my heavenly patron was with me the whole way. I am grateful to him for basically punching me in the mouth on the eve of his feast, and then sticking with me until the habit was kicked. There's more to the story, read under Prayer 6.

Thank you St. Jude Thaddeus!

4. The Great Jude Thaddeus Prayer
Version A

Most holy Apostle, St. Jude Thaddeus, faithful servant and friend of Jesus, the name of the traitor who delivered your beloved Master into the hands of His enemies has caused you to be forgotten by many, but the Church honors and invokes you universally as the patron of hopeless cases and of things despaired of. Pray for me, I am so miserable; make use, I implore you, of that particular privilege accorded to you to bring visible and speedy help where help is almost despaired of. Come to my assistance in this great need that I may receive the consolations and help of heaven in all my necessities, tribula-

tions, and sufferings, particularly (*here make your request*) and that I bless God with you and all the elect throughout eternity.

I promise you, O blessed Jude, to be forever mindful of this great favor, and I will never cease to honor you as my special and powerful patron and to do all in my power to encourage devotion to you. Amen.

This is my "big one." This is the first prayer to St. Jude I learned back when I was a freshman in high school; it is also the prayer to him I use every day in conjunction with the Rosary. How the prayer appears above is how it is worded, with only minor variations, in most material printed about Jude Thaddeus since the early 20th century . However, I discovered a version of it that dates back to 1826, from an out-of-print work called the *Officium Parvum* or *Little Office of St. Jude*. It is this work which first specifically mentions the Apostle as "the special advocate of the unfortunate and well-nigh hopeless."[18] The prayer was translated from Latin to English by Fr. Paul Stenhouse, God rest his soul.[19] It is the oldest non-liturgical prayer to St. Jude of which I am aware:

Version B

Most holy Apostle, most faithful servant and friend of Christ, Jude Thaddeus, who shares the same name as the betrayer of Jesus and on that account may not be honored as is your right. Because of your most holy and apostolic life you have been called upon as an advocate by the True Church in times of calamity and desperation. Pray for me to God in my time of trial. Through your merits may I receive consolation in my tribulations and difficulties. May I experience God's help, and yours especially in my present plight and straitened circumstances. Finally, at the hour of my death, along with you and all the saints, may I love and bless the eternal God. Amen.

For my personal prayer, I have adapted and harmonized the two versions. (For what it's worth, I also translated it into my ancestral language, *Gaeilg*, i.e. Irish, which is the only language I conduct my personal prayers in. I have published the prayers here in English, for obvious reasons).

Version C

Most holy Apostle, Jude Thaddeus, most faithful servant, friend, and kinsman of Christ, you share the same name as the betrayer of Jesus and on that account may not have been honored as is your right. Because of your most holy and apostolic life you have been called upon as an advocate by the True Church in times of calamity and desperation. Pray for me to God in my time of trial; make use, I implore you, of that particular privilege accorded to you to bring visible and speedy help where help is almost despaired of. Through your merits may I receive consolation in my tribulations, difficulties, and sufferings. May I experience God's help and yours, especially in my present plight and straitened circumstances, particularly (*here make your request*). Finally, at the hour of my death, along with you and all the saints, may I love and bless the eternal God.

I promise you, O blessed Jude, to be forever mindful of this great favor, and to never cease honoring you as my special and powerful patron, and to do all in my power to encourage devotion to you. Amen.

The prayers in this chapter are holy, but they were not spoken by Jesus Christ Himself like the Our Father was. So, you can adapt them to your personal needs in your private devotions. For instance, in this prayer I typically say "these great needs" instead of the usual "this great need." And in the *here make your request* section, I have a list of intentions about triple the length of the prayer itself. Yes, I have quite the list of hopeless causes!

But St. Jude does not ever disappoint me, thanks be to God.

5. Daily Prayer in Desperate Times

O glorious Apostle, St. Jude, true relative of Jesus and Mary, I salute you through the Most Sacred Heart of Jesus. I praise and thank God for all the graces He has bestowed upon you. I implore you, through the Sacred Heart of Jesus, to look upon me with compassion; despise not my poor prayer and let not my trust be in vain. To you has been assigned the privilege of aiding us in the most desperate cases. Come to my aid that I may praise the mercies of God. All my life, I will be grateful to you and will be your faithful client until I can thank you in heaven. Amen.

The Sacred Heart of Jesus burns with the most intense love for mankind. The devotion to St. Jude Thaddeus is intimately connected with the devotion to the Sacred Heart, because it is precisely in the loving "purity of his heart" and not his family relationship that Thaddeus resembles Jesus Christ. This prayer capitalizes on that connection. It is ultimately the infinitely merciful love of our only Master and Lord that will bring us safely through the most desperate times.

6. Prayer in the Face of Illness

Dear Apostle and martyr for Christ, you left us an Epistle in the New Testament. With good reason many invoke you when illness is at a desperate stage. We now recommend to your kindness (*here state the name of patient*) who is in critical condition. May the cure of (this patient) increase his/her faith and love for the Lord of Life, for the glory of our merciful God. Amen.

Medical issues are a specific domain for which St. Jude's intercessory powers are especially trusted by those who call upon him. In fact, according to the academic study *Thank You, St. Jude*, over half of all the letters received by his Chicago shrine concerned illness.[20] This proportion held steady throughout the 20th century .

It is no wonder then, that the most famous institution in the world dedicated to him is a hospital, St. Jude Children's Research Hospital in Memphis, Tennessee. The sad sinful state of the human race leaves us susceptible to every form of sickness, disease, and physical distress. The loving Jude Thaddeus is eager to pull us out of the depths of despair that such ailments can put us in.

Of course, if you are the one who happens to be sick, you can adapt the wording to reflect that. For instance, "May the cure of (this patient) increase his/her faith…" can become, "May the cure of my ailment increase my faith…," or something like that.

By the way, here's what happened with the extreme mouth pain I described under Prayer 3. On St. Thaddeus Day, August 21, 2020, I reached out to Fr. Patrick Maloney, a legendary and holy Melkite Catholic priest from Ireland. It had been on my mind for a while to visit him in his downtown Manhattan home; I had not seen him in some years. We set up a meeting and made it happen sometime in the following week. Incidentally, this was to be my first time back in my native city since the beginning of the year, and a lot had changed in a short time – pandemic, riots, urban decay. But Fr. Pat had not fled; he was as indefatigable as ever.

When I visited, we chatted for hours. I had a dentist's appointment the next day and the intense pain had not yet abated. I asked him for the sacrament of the Anointing of the Sick, to which he graciously agreed. We went upstairs to his chapel for the administration of the sacrament. It all went exactly as described in the Epistle of Jude's brother James (5:14-15). Well, what did I see up on the chapel wall but an icon of St. Jude Thaddeus, prominently mounted above icons of the Gaelic saints Pádraig and Bríd (Patrick and Bridget)!

From that day on, the pain went down, eventually disappearing. I did visit the dentist the next day. The physical misery was already much reduced by the time I saw him, but his professional concern was that it would get worse. While I appreciated his empathy, he didn't need to worry himself because it did not get worse.

Please do not construe any of this to mean I am advocating for ignoring medical professionals. Quite the opposite – take their advice seriously. God gave them knowledge and abilities according to His will. The dentist had identified an underlying problem that needed a root canal. I had to wait a month for an appointment, but I did it. That was a long time to wait for the agony to stop, but to everyone's surprise, the pain went away on its own from the time I received the Anointing under Thaddeus' loving gaze.

The Anointing of the Sick is not guaranteed to always bring physical healing, according to God's perfect and holy will. But it *always* accomplishes the far more astounding feat of bringing healing to the soul.

All I am doing here is relating what I experienced first hand while writing this book. You can't make this stuff up. Glory to God, blessed be Mary the Theotokos, and thank you St. Jude Thaddeus – again!

7. In Grievous Affliction

O St. Jude Thaddeus, relative of Jesus Christ, glorious Apostle and martyr, renowned for your virtues and miracles, faithful and prompt intercessor of all who honor and trust in you! You are a powerful patron and helper in grievous afflictions. I come to you and entreat you from the depths of my heart; come to my aid with your powerful intercession, for you have received from God the privilege to assist with your manifest help those who almost despair of all hope.

Look down upon me; my life is a life of crosses, my days are days of tribulation, and my heart is an ocean of bitterness. All my paths are strewn with thorns and scarcely one moment passes but is witness of my tears and sighs; uneasiness, discouragement, mistrust, and near despair prey upon my soul.

Please, you cannot forsake me in this sad plight. I will not depart from you until you have heard me. O hasten to my aid! I will be grateful to you all my life. I will honor you as my special patron, I will thank God for the graces bestowed upon you, and will encourage devotion to you according to my power. Amen.

St. Jude Thaddeus, pray for all who invoke your aid.

If there is any circumstance in which St. Jude is most suited to help us, it's precisely when we are in grievous affliction. Who you gonna call? Not Ghostbusters – that is a fun idea but fictional, and in any case ghosts are unlikely to be a problem for most people. In real life, call

Heaven's 9-1-1 to reach St. Jude Thaddeus! "He will show himself most willing to give help,"[21] as our Lord told St. Birgitta of Sweden.

Call on him, then look for signs of encouragement. Heaven speaks to us through signs and symbols in the natural universe which God created for our benefit. St. Paul lays it out like this: "Ever since the creation of the world his [God's] invisible nature, namely, his eternal power and deity, has been clearly perceived in the things that have been made" (Rom 1:20). Keep your eyes and ears open and don't worry. **Help is on the way**.

Just remember the story Christ told us of the window and the judge (Lk 18:1-8).

Note that this prayer closes with us asking him to help everyone who calls upon him. We are all in this together, so Christian love demands that we be generous with our prayer. And all of us who call upon St. Jude Thaddeus have an automatic spiritual bond with one another , brought together by our common devotion to our heavenly patron. It's a pretty cool thing that just as you are praying for other devotees of Jude who you don't know, they are also praying for you.

8. For Spiritual Help

St. Jude Thaddeus, glorious Apostle, martyr, and relative of Jesus, you spread the true faith among the most barbarous and distant nations, and won to the obedience of Jesus Christ many tribes and peoples by the power of His holy word. Grant, I beseech you, that from this day I may renounce every sinful habit, be preserved from all evil thoughts, and always obtain your assistance, particularly in every danger and difficulty. May I safely reach our heavenly home

and with you adore the most holy Trinity, Father, Son, and Holy Spirit, forever and ever. Amen.

Recall that St. Bernard credited St. Jude's intercession with preserving his purity. Jude has a particular focus on helping us to be worthy of this promise of Christ: "Blessed are the pure in heart, for they shall see God" (Mt 5:8). As we know, Jude himself was pure in heart. This is why he earned the name Thaddeus, and more importantly, earned the right to see God with a clarity in proportion to his heart's purity.

There are solid grounds for considering habitual sexual sins as hopeless and desperate cases. So many fall into these sins with great ease because of the distorted attractions of our fallen nature, and the consequent obsessions of thought and behavior can be very difficult to break. And early 21st century society does not make it any easier with its rampant and easily accessible pornography.

On the other hand, this unfortunate societal situation is simultaneously a great opportunity for heroic virtue. The very fact that this kind of sin is so effortless to delve into and so generally accepted in mainstream culture makes avoiding it for the sake of God's kingdom all the more brave, gutsy, and meritorious. And, crucial for our salvation.

9. The St. Jude Novena Prayer

To St. Jude, holy St. Jude, Apostle and martyr, great in virtue and rich in miracles, near kinsman of Jesus Christ, faithful intercessor of all who invoke your special patronage in time of need. To you I have recourse from the depths of my heart and humbly beg to whom God has given such great power to come to my assistance. Help me in my present and urgent petition; in return I promise to make your name

known and cause you to be invoked. St. Jude pray for us and all who invoke your aid. Amen.

The practice known as the "novena" is one of the most hallowed traditions of popular piety in Christendom. Basically, say the prayer for nine days in a row. For greater effectiveness, say it in conjunction with the other great prayers, as per what we've already discussed. And for the greatest effectiveness, offer your petitions in union with Christ on the Cross in the Eucharist.

The practice of praying novenas was developed and preserved in the Latin Catholic tradition, but they can be used to good effect by anybody seeking God in confidence. Indeed, the roots of the novena go back to the very beginning of the Catholic Church. Our Lord rose from the dead on Easter Sunday and stayed around in physically recognizable form for forty days. Just before He returned to His Father in heaven on Ascension Thursday, He commanded His Apostles, Jude among them, to wait for Him to send the Holy Spirit. The Spirit was to be sent to them on Pentecost Sunday, the day recognized as the birthday of the Church.

The Apostles returned to Jerusalem and went into the upper room in the place where they were staying. There were exactly nine days in between Ascension Thursday and Pentecost. During this time St. Jude and the Apostles, "with one accord devoted themselves to prayer, together with the women and Mary the mother of Jesus, and with his brethren" (Acts 1:14).

These nine days of prayer are the origin of the novena, so by praying one we are following a practice that Jude Thaddeus helped to originate. I would also like to point out that the Rosary is a particularly good set of prayers to say with a novena so that we can be of one accord with the Mother of God, who was with the Apostles in the upper room.

You will notice that all these prayers have us offering to make Jude's name known and honored, as if that is something he wants. And he does. In fact, this has been an intrinsic part of the devotion from its earliest days. St. Jude wants to be invoked so that he can share the Good News that will bring you to Christ – that is, to bring you to the fulfillment of the deep-seated human yearning for true happiness. Since this was so important to Jude Thaddeus that he devoted the whole latter part of his life to sharing the Gospel, even to the point of giving up his life for it, we can be confident that he is continuing this mission in heaven.

10. To Obtain Divine Wisdom and Love

O glorious St. Jude Thaddeus, by those sublime privileges which so ennobled you in your lifetime – your relationship according to the flesh with our Lord Jesus Christ, and your vocation to the apostolate – by that glory, which, as the reward of your labor and martyrdom, you now enjoy in heaven, obtain for me, from the giver of all good things, the spiritual and temporal favors I need.

Enable me to acquire the treasury of that divinely inspired doctrine which you have written about in your own biblical Epistle. Help me to raise on high the edifice of perfection upon the foundation of the faith, by prayer and the help of the Holy Spirit. Enable me to keep myself always in the love of God, waiting upon the mercy of Jesus Christ for eternal life, and to help by every available means those who stray from the truth.

Thus shall I exalt the glory, the majesty, the dominion, the might of Him who can preserve me from sin, and keep me stainless

and joyous for the coming of my Lord Jesus Christ, my divine Savior. Amen.

This is a great prayer to say before reading the Epistle of St. Jude, or at any time to help you live out his teachings. You will see that this prayer actually replicates much of the wording of the biblical letter. You cannot go wrong with words that are directly inspired by the Holy Spirit of God.

St. Jude's Epistle is so short, yet so profoundly sublime. It serves as a great introduction to the Gospel message in a similar way to how the St. Jude devotion serves as a great introduction to a true life of Christian prayer. But the short biblical letter is very easy to gloss over if it's only given a cursory read. Unlocking its treasures can thus be an intellectual and spiritual challenge.

This prayer can help with that. You would be talking to the Epistle's human author himself! And he hears you, and will help you gain understanding and wisdom from the divine Author. I think that that's pretty cool – I love books, and really love the idea of talking to the authors to gain a better understanding. I sometimes have had the opportunity to speak to writers I admire, and it is always an edifying experience. There are many other authors who I have yet to meet, and others I will never meet in this life because they're dead. And once they are passed from this life we usually do not know their eternal fate.

But we do know in the case of St. Jude. He is really and truly alive with our Lord and **a)** he hears us **b)** he cares **c)** he has been granted by Jesus the special privilege of helping us in difficult circumstances. With this prayer we are talking to the author of the work we are perusing. We are actually talking to a *real* celebrity. And we are also talking to his boss, our God, the greatest celebrity of all.

And, the petitions of this prayer will absolutely be granted. The Holy Spirit tells us so, through Jude's brother James: "If any of you lacks wisdom, let him ask God, who gives to all men generously and without reproaching, and it will be given him" (1:5).

There you have it – pray this prayer with faith and persistence, and what you ask for will be yours. Christ tells us this about prayer in general, but in this case we are explicitly and specifically asking for wisdom (and by extension, the supernatural love from which it is inseparable).

Amen!

11. Litany of St. Jude Thaddeus

Lord, have mercy on us!

Christ, have mercy on us!

Lord, have mercy on us!

Christ, hear us!

Christ, graciously hear us!

God, the Father of heaven, have mercy on us!

God, the Son, Redeemer of the world, have mercy on us!

God, the Holy Spirit, have mercy on us!

Holy Trinity, one God, have mercy on us!

St. Jude, relative of Jesus and Mary, pray for us!

St. Jude, raised to the dignity of an Apostle, pray for us!

St. Jude, who had the honor of beholding your Divine Master St. Jude, while on earth deemed worthy to see Jesus and Mary and to enjoy their company, pray for us! humble Himself to wash your feet, pray for us!

St. Jude, who at the Last Supper did receive the first Holy Communion in history from the hands of Jesus, pray for us!

St. Jude, who after the profound grief which the death of your beloved Master caused you, had the consolation of beholding Him risen from the dead, and of assisting at His glorious Ascension, pray for us!

St. Jude, who was filled with the Holy Spirit on the day of Pentecost, pray for us!

St. Jude, who did preach the Gospel in the land of Israel, in Assyria, in Persia, and in Armenia, pray for us!

St. Jude, who did convert many people to the Faith, pray for us!

St. Jude, who did perform wonderful miracles in the power of the Holy Spirit, pray for us!

St. Jude, who did restore an idolatrous king to health, both of soul and body, pray for us!

St. Jude, who did impose silence on demons, and confound their oracles, pray for us!

St. Jude, who did foretell to a weak prince an honorable peace with his powerful enemy, pray for us!

St. Jude, who did take from deadly serpents the power of injuring man, pray for us!

St. Jude, who disregarding the threats of the impious, did courageously preach the doctrine of Christ, pray for us!

St. Jude, who did gloriously suffer martyrdom for the love of your Divine Master, pray for us!

Blessed Apostle, with confidence, we invoke you!

Blessed Apostle, with confidence, we invoke you!

St. Jude, help of the hopeless, aid us in our distress!

St. Thaddeus, help of the hopeless, aid us in our distress!

St. Jude, help of the hopeless, aid us in our distress!

That by your intercession both priests and people of the Church may obtain an ardent zeal for the Faith of Jesus Christ, we beseech you, hear us!

That you would defend our Sovereign Pontiff and obtain peace and unity for the Holy Church, we beseech you, hear us!

That faith, hope, and love may increase in our hearts, we beseech you, hear us!

That we may be delivered from all evil thoughts, and from all the snares of the devil, we beseech you, hear us!

That you would graciously grant aid and protection to all who honor you, we beseech you, hear us!

That you would preserve us from all sin and from all occasion of sin, we beseech you, hear us!

That you would defend us at the hour of death, against the fury of the devil and his evil spirits, we beseech you, hear us!

Lamb of God, who takes away the sins of the world, spare us, O Lord.

Lamb of God, who takes away the sins of the world, graciously hear us, O Lord.

Lamb of God, who takes away the sins of the world, have mercy on us.

Pray for us, Blessed Jude Thaddeus,

That we be made worthy of the promises of Christ.

This kind of long form call-and-response prayer is known as a litany. The 1910 *Catholic Encyclopedia* tells us that, "a litany is a well-known and much appreciated form of responsive petition, used in public liturgical services, and in private devotions."[22] Litanies are of ancient provenance; the prototype is Psalm 136 (135). This psalm begins with, "O give thanks to the LORD, for he is good, for his mercy endures for ever." It then goes through a series of one-line praises of God's glory and deeds, each with the response, "for his mercy endures forever."

St. Jude Thaddeus, the amiable and loving one, is an Apostle who is especially linked to our Lord's Sacred Heart of Divine Mercy. It is thus sublimely appropriate to call upon him in supplication with this form of prayer which is modeled on the ancient biblical praise of the Lord's mercy.

9

Gratitude And Giving Back

Beyond Thank You

I am so confident that St. Jude Thaddeus will amaze you with his heavenly help that I have written an entire chapter about the thanksgiving portion of the devotion. Peppered throughout the book are stories of petitions to God's first responder getting answered. This chapter deals with what to do in the aftermath of such visibly successful intercession. Let's begin with the twelfth prayer, which I saved for this chapter to start it off on the right foot.

12. Prayer of Thanksgiving (When a Favor Has Been Granted)

O most sweet Lord Jesus Christ, in union with the unutterable heavenly praise with which the Most Holy Trinity extols itself and which thence flows upon your Sacred Humanity, upon Mary, upon all the angels and saints, I praise, glorify, and bless you for all the graces and privileges you have bestowed upon your chosen Apostle and intimate friend, St. Jude Thaddeus. I pray to you, for the sake of his

merits, grant me your grace, and through his intercession come to my aid in all my needs, but especially at the hour of my death deign to strengthen against the rage of my enemies. Amen.

Our Father, Hail Mary, Glory Be – Three times.

According to the scholarly book *Thank You St. Jude!*, it was implicitly understood that those who received favors were to pay him back in some way.[23] This kind of payback is born of gratitude, a free gift to Jude as a token. It's not that he needs it. Jude is enjoying the eternal glory of heaven, he sees the face of God forever, and he has absolutely no need to be concerned with our earthly affairs. But he does concern himself, because he is filled with the selfless love so characteristic of his personality that he was bestowed with the name Thaddeus.

We really do not need an academic study to tell us that gratitude should move us to act, spurring us to perform some action which recognizably expresses thanks. It is a natural law of human behavior that is clearly seen in operation in every culture and in every era of history. We receive freely and so we give freely, even though we cannot possibly give as good as we get. Fear not, this is quite the opposite of a "deal with the devil." The *cultus* of St. Jude Thaddeus is one hundred percent good and holy.

You really did not think you would get something for nothing, did you? Ha! Come on now. But it's okay, you will be so blown away with our saint's incomparable prowess that grateful acts will quite naturally flow out of you.

Alas, it is true that there are people who will just take, take, take. They take and never reciprocate. I have witnessed such behavior and I'm sure you have, too. Unfortunately, this happens with the St. Jude devotion itself. There are those who have received great favors after calling upon Jude but who do not follow up with anything of substance to show gratitude. They might just throw him a "Thank you for your service," which is good as far as it goes, but is hollow and useless if it is not backed up.

One contrite devotee, named Joshua, publicly acknowledged the error of his own sloth: "I apologize for my prior arrogance and not thanking you for all your previous blessings you've bestowed on me and my family throughout the years... My good fortune is possible because of your blessings, Thank you again for all you do."[24] Fortunately, he made up for his previous negligence.

In reality, there is nothing we can really do to reciprocate St. Jude's generosity. As has been pointed out, he already has everything he could possibly need or want – he is with God in eternal glory! But the idea is that we on earth need to have the proper emotional disposition, and this is for our own good.

Shock and Awe

By the very nature of the particular scope of his intercessory powers, concerning that of petitions described as hopeless or impossible, it is almost inevitable that a sense of wonder would result from the granting of a petition. That is, because the petitioner is asking for something that is so unlikely in the first place, when it is granted he or she is very likely to be overwhelmed with astonishment. Shock and awe, so to speak. We can see where God would like for things to go from this point.

Ideally, an answered prayer should increase faith and cultivate an "attitude of gratitude," as the cliché goes. Yes, God wants us to tell people the Gospel, the Good News! In fact, he commands us to, "go into all the world and preach the gospel to the whole creation" (Mk 16:15).

Grateful people who have had their lives touched in such remarkable ways tend to tell others. For instance, when Christ cured a leper at the very beginning of his public ministry, He put him under strict orders not to tell anyone. The grateful cured leper did not listen and "went out and began to talk freely about it, and to spread the news so that Jesus could no longer openly enter a town, but was out in the country; and people came to him from every quarter" (Mk 1:45).

Well, if someone's jubilation over the granting of a favor caused him to disregard an injunction of the Messiah Himself, how much more would our thanksgiving go viral if there were no such injunction! And in fact, there is no such injunction nowadays; the opposite holds true – we are to spread the news.

As we see with the cured leper above, it was a grateful man who told everyone in his orbit about the wonderful goodness this Jesus did for him. It was this that made the Lord a "rock star" in the eyes of the Galileans. The celebrity buzz, in turn, facilitated the attention of the masses being directed to this new public figure and for the eventual revelation of His true identity and message.

When Jesus grants us wonderful favors through his friend Jude, let's tell people! Actually, this is why I wrote *Heaven Help Us, Now!* in the first place – it was born out of love and gratitude for St. Jude's timely intercession in protecting my wife and daughter during a very rough time. But we got through, thank you St. Jude!

Show Him Gratitude

There are so many tangible ways to show St. Jude Thaddeus that we are grateful for his help. Here are some of them:

1. **TELL** people verbally. This is the oldest method in the book. Way back in the Stone Age, before writing and money were invented, people had their voices. In fact, the human language faculty is part of our genetic inheritance. It is basic and intrinsic. And we are social creatures who live in interconnected webs of relationships through which information is most intimately disseminated. Let your voice be heard!

2. **RECORD** a voice or video message. Perhaps share it with your friends and family, or perhaps put it out in a public forum. Recording your testimonial about St. Jude will allow it to reach and influence more people.

3. **WRITE** a letter, send an email, put out a social media post. Writing has a permanence that the spoken word does not, and thus has a potential reach and longevity that is unmatched for sharing a message. Just look at the Bible!

4. **GIFT** this book to people. The express purpose of *Heaven Help Us, Now!* is to explain the St. Jude Thaddeus devotion to a whole new generation. If you feel a bit bashful about speaking to people yourself, I understand. Or if you just want a competent wingman, I get it. That's what this book is for.

5. **DONATE** to a worthy cause, particularly one linked to St. Jude. Even if it's just a little bit, you could have a positive impact far beyond what one might expect, like the poor widow and the two coins (Mk 12:41-44). A list of holy places associated with him is in Chapter 4. Donating to them will not only help out a worthy cause, but it will also be of great profit to your soul.

6. **PRAY** for others. This is an act of mercy which pleases God and costs nothing but the time and attention required to do it. But it should come rather naturally to anyone devoted to St. Jude. If you are already praying for others, especially for your loved ones, consider praying for people you can't stand! The Lord loves when we pray for our enemies (Mt 5:43-48).

Really Show Him Gratitude

There are certainly many ways to show gratitude. But the greatest way to show gratitude and to ensure the greatest likelihood of a favorable outcome to your petition is to *follow Jude's teachings* with the same open mind and open heart with which you turned to him in the first place.

The Gospel is a whole and unified entity, but each apostolic teacher puts emphasis on particular aspects of it. Fortunately, St. Jude has left us a record of part of his teachings, *The Catholic Epistle of St. Jude the Apostle*, as the revered Douay-Rheims translation calls it. Other titles it goes by are *The Letter of Jude* and *The Book of Jude*. It is a book in the sense that each biblical work when taken individually is known as a "book," regardless of length. It is the final epistle in the New Testament and the second to last book of the Bible, coming right before Revelation (Apocalypse). It is also the second shortest work in the New Testament.

God gave St. Jude a very special honor by allowing him to be one of the human authors of the Bible. It is a singular privilege to have one's work included in the canon of Holy Scripture, a privilege reserved to apostolic writers – that is, to authors from the first generation of Christianity who have been identified by the Church as having produced specific works under the inspiration of the Holy Spirit. They were all Apostles themselves or working directly under the authority of the Apostles.

We might be able to glean a bit more of the Apostle Jude's mind from the theology contained in the *Anaphora of Addai and Mari* and from the legendary tidbits caught by the ancient historian Eusebius and his like. These exceptions aside, we do not know much else of St. Jude Thaddeus' teaching during his life on earth. But we can be certain that this letter is the portion of his teaching that God wished all generations to have access to, because it made it into the Bible.

To lead people to Christ is Jude's greatest wish. It is apparent in his numerous references to Christ in his short letter – six times in all. The frequency of Jude's use of Jesus' messianic appellation relative to the length of the work is matched by no other New Testament writer except Paul.[25]

And so the greatest way to pay St. Jude Thaddeus back is to pay greater attention to following the Gospel of Christ. And following the Gospel opens you to the mercy of Jesus Christ when it's our turn for Him to judge us.

Catch-22 Makes Us Happy

St. Jude Thaddeus touches our lives in such profound ways that it is only natural that our joy will shine through and get the attention of others. This is our chance to say something! The first Pope tells us exactly what to do and how: "Always be prepared to make a defense to any one who calls you to account for the hope that is in you, yet do it with gentleness and reverence" (1 Pt 2:15). The demeanor that St. Peter calls for is common sense for dealing with people on most matters, but is particularly pertinent when discussing the faith.

We usually have to talk to people to spread the Gospel, but sometimes merely mentioning the Gospel makes people stop talking to us! It's a bit of a catch 22, right? Well, that's just the way it is. God set up the world in such a way as to make anything worthwhile involve effort and ingenuity to accomplish. We should be grateful to Him and glorify Him for blessing us with such challenges. But keeping ourselves in the faith is in fact a challenge, never mind helping others to come to it.

Here's a bit of unconventional advice on that: **Have fun!** Life and death are some serious matters, to put it mildly. But the Lord gave us the ability to derive value out of challenges. If we have the peace of Christ in us, there is no reason we can't tackle the challenge of spreading the Gospel with joy, humor, and playfulness. In fact, our infectious enthusiasm is undoubtedly far more effective in communicating the Good News than being a sour, dour sad sack. Enthusiasm has a contagious quality because it is just so darn attractive.

Madoc: A Mystery is an epic book-length work by the Irish poet Paul Muldoon. It is delightfully intricate, richly textured with wordplay and allusion, and just a bit obscure. It was quite a feat to write. Yet, it was a joy for Muldoon. "Or, as Muldoon himself says, more cryptically: 'I quite enjoy having fun. It's part of how it is, and who we are.'"[26] Yes, I like how he puts it. It conveys the spirit of what I'm talking about.

I think everyone can recognize that just about everything in life requires some kind of effort. This is just the way God set things up when Adam and Eve were kicked out of Eden, "in the sweat of your face you shall eat bread" (Gn 3:19). But we can do penance for our sins, store up treasure in heaven *and* gain a sense of competency and mastery in the here-and-now by overcoming challenges in spreading the word. So, I say again: while telling people your personal testimony of how St. Jude has helped you, **have fun!**

Sheep in Wolves' Clothing

Christ spoke of wolves in sheep's clothing (Mt 7:15). Perhaps there is also such a thing as sheep in wolves' clothing. One of the spiritual challenges that God presents to us is that the Good News is spread by imperfect messengers. Yet, this is how the Lord willed it. He could easily manifest Himself openly and individually to each and every human on earth. But He doesn't. I, for one, think that this is just plain awesome for no other reason than it's God's plan. It's His will so it must be good.

But it is the plain reality that the sheep are often hidden by wolves' clothing. A case in point is the dubious legacy of the Roman Empire. Simon Peter chose to spend his last days in Rome, which forevermore became the capital of Christianity. But Rome was also the capital of an empire which engaged in the most sickening and evil debauchery, and whose armies had no problem engaging in genocide.

One could make the argument that all that bad stuff predated the Church. The problem is that the same holds true for polities that appeared after the Church gained ascendancy, for instance, the Spanish and Portuguese Empires of more recent centuries. Actually, my blood boils when I think of the *conquistadores* laughing as they committed acts of murder and rape so gruesome that I don't feel comfortable detailing them here.

And yet, these latter-day empires claimed to be Christian. What makes things even more twisted is that they actually did facilitate the spread of holiness and the preaching of the Gospel. The heartbreaking stories of imperial atrocities do not take away from the selfless saintly work of Spanish and Portuguese missionaries who brought eternal life to multitudes. The weeds and the wheat were truly mixed in with each oth-er (Mt 13:24-30).

We must keep the weeds and the wheat distinct in our minds and help others to do so. It takes mental vigilance; the devil is continuously working at confusing us into error. This is why the Catholic Church has been the victim of "fake news" stories for a good two thousand years or so. The sad fact is that no amount of truth and goodness will eliminate the vitriolic evil of those who stand with the devil (at least not until our Lord returns in glory). However, there are many people of good will who could be reached if only we make clear that we are the wheat and not the weeds, that we are Jesus' sheep and not Satan's wolves!

How Much Can You Handle?

Some people might be worried about not being able to handle the burden of telling others how St. Jude helped them, never mind spreading the full Gospel of Christ. Indeed, not everyone can handle such a task. But don't worry. God won't give you what you can't handle. St. Paul tells us, "God is faithful, and he will not let you be tempted beyond your strength, but with the temptation will also provide the way of escape that you may be able to endure it" (1 Cor 10:13).

But wait – isn't that a contradiction? If God will not give us what we cannot handle, how is it that there are people who can't handle things?

Because we will in fact crack up, break down, and be completely overwhelmed *if we rely **only** on our own strength*.

But if we draw our strength from the lifeline that is Jesus Christ, it is only then that we will pass the test, maybe even get an A+. Jesus lays it bare: "I am the vine, you are the branches ... apart from me you can do nothing" (Jn 15:5). This is such an important point that He includes the invocation of spiritual protection as one of the seven petitions to our Father who art in heaven: "And lead us not into temptation" (Mt 6:13).

Jesus includes this as a petition because the free will He gave us necessitates that we call upon Him voluntarily; we have to ask Him. Our Lord explicates, "Watch and pray that you may not enter into temptation; the spirit is indeed willing, but the flesh is weak (Mk 14:38).

Jesus has given us St. Jude Thaddeus as one of His most powerful secret weapons to help us overcome adversity. Jude is that fireman who snatches up the terrified child who was just about to be consumed by the raging inferno of a burning building. Just when we are at our weakest, he rides in to the rescue to preserve our lifeline to Christ.

Just *ask him* to help. That's **all it takes to start!**

Use Your Christmas Present!

Remember that Christmas, the Nativity of our Lord, is Jesus' birthday. Of course, we all know this. But there is tremendous symbolism in the most prominent of Christmas customs, the giving of gifts. God gifted His only Son to us, in the flesh, made visible to the world on this day.

God wants to give you things, and he *has* already given you much. But He wants to give you more. This famous scripture quote says it all: "For God so loved the world that he sent his only-begotten Son, that whoever believes in him should not perish but have eternal life" (Jn 3:16). If that does not speak to God's unfathomable generosity, I don't know what does. He doesn't just want us to live, He wants us to *really* live. "I came that they may have life, and have it abundantly" (Jn 10:10).

Free will is one of these great gifts He has given us. It is the tool by which we make the choices that allow us access to the abundant life the Lord is leading us to. It is thus a necessary component of achieving the perfection He wants to give us. Notice that the Bible tells us that "whoever believes in him" is the one who will get the reward. In other words, faith is not passive – we actively *choose* to believe with our free will.

And we prove to Him that our belief is real by *choosing* to live a life in accordance with *His* will. We are not talking about the mere belief in God's existence, but *faith*, the loving acceptance of His message. He tells us, "If you love me, you will keep my commandments" (Jn 14:15). The Book of Sirach (15:15) perfectly sums up this fundamental concept: "If you *will* [emphasis added] you can keep the commandments, they will save you; / if you trust in God, you too shall live."

We all know that there are presents each year that do not actually get used. They get put away, given away, returned to the shop, whatever. Please do not do that with your free will! It is exceptionally powerful but can be misused by being unused.

How can free will be unused? Don't people by nature do what they want to do?

Well, I'm glad you asked. If we blindly follow our emotionalistic animal passions we are, in effect, disabling our capacity to choose freely. St. Jude writes powerfully about this in his biblical letter. Think of a drug or alcohol addict who follows the cravings of his body to do bad things to himself and to others. He did not necessarily set out to be a bad person. In fact, people who love him can usually testify to his loveable qualities.

But when we make an initial decision with our free will not to use free will by putting our impulsive cravings in the driver's seat, a recipe for tragedy is created.

Those who use the powerful help of St. Jude Thaddeus have the power of the universe at their disposal. They freely choose the good, and they know that no matter how hard life can be, they will WIN. They made the right *choice*.

Lukewarm – *Eww!*

I feel duty-bound to give a sincere warning about being a deadbeat with regard to expressing proper gratitude to God. If we are outright evil, He is filled with the greatest pity and concern to save us. If we're on fire with love for Him, He loves that, of course. But if we are in between, just unmotivated lumps of clay, fluttering along in life with no concern for deep and grand things… well, He *despises* lukewarmness with regard to the gift of the faith.

I'm not joking. This is what Jesus tells us: "I know your works: you are neither cold nor hot. Would that you were cold or hot! So, because you are lukewarm and neither cold nor hot, I will spew you out of my mouth" (Rv 3:15-16).

He spoke that to St. John back in the 1st century He has not changed His view; Jesus reiterated His stance to St. Faustina in the 20th century: "My soul suffered the most dreadful loathing in the Garden of Olives because of lukewarm souls … Souls without love or devotion, souls full of egoism and selfishness … lukewarm souls with just enough warmth to keep themselves alive: My Heart cannot bear this … I cannot stand them because they are neither good nor bad."[27] Okay then. Even now as I write this I am taking in the heavy import of Christ's words.

Dear Lord, You have made Yourself quite clear. I beg you to never allow my passion for you to abate, and to continually increase my faith and my zeal for it.

I do believe that gratitude comes naturally to most people who have been gifted something of value. But we are human and we can be a bit dense. So, being reminded of how the Lord detests lukewarmness of heart can be a good kick in the pants for us to stay on our game.

God, being the One who designed us, knows we have the capacity to change our attitudes. In fact, we are only judged by what we freely choose, not our natural looks or DNA or what family we're born into. The more free our choice is, the more responsible we are for it and its results. "This freedom characterizes properly human acts. It is *the basis* [emphasis added] of praise or blame, merit or reproach" (CCC 1732). If we are judged *only* on what we do with our free will, but we are also judged for the zeal of our faith, it logically follows that the zeal of our faith is inside the bounds of our free will. Our level of belief and enthusiasm for that belief is thus within the parameters of what we consciously control, of what we choose of our own volition.

So, let's not be lukewarm! (Eww, yuk, who really wants to be vomited out in disgust by the Supreme Being).

Instead, let's be grateful to the Lord and to His servant St. Jude Thaddeus for letting us experience just a tiny bit of the joy of heaven by getting us out of whatever desperate jam we were in.

A Quality of (Eternal) Life Issue

Here is another bit of motivation to keep you on the gratitude train.

One thing that is not negotiable with God is that you have one mortal life. That's it, one and only one. When you're dead you're done, at least insofar as being saved or damned. Oh, you get plenty of second chances; that's the beauty of time. Unlike the fallen angels who fell for all eternity, if we make a mistake, if we sin, we can make amends with God in linear time. There's a before and after, a past, present, and future. This life on earth *is* the second chance! We have any number of opportunities, on any day and at any time. I think it would be quite foolish to:

1) Reject the generous way that God set things up, by thinking, "Oh, I'm a good person, I don't need it." It is safer and more Christian to think in the following manner:

> "Am I *really* a good person? After all, there are two considerations –
> a. Who am I to judge? I can examine my conscience, but I have no authority to *judge* if I am a good person. Only God is the judge. He alone will give me plaudits if I deserve them; in the meantime, stay humble.
> b. I need to get off my high horse! – no one is truly good but God. Jesus, who is both good and God, was so humble in his earthly ministry that He rejected being called 'good teacher'" (A reference to Lk 18:18-19).

2) Wasting His mercy by being lazy or lackadaisical about living life according to the Gospel. Not only do lukewarm people induce nausea in Jesus (Rv 3:16), but you just do not know when your time is going to run out (Mk 13:32-37).

This life matters not only for the binary choice of heaven or hell, but for the particular kind of eternal glory, or lack thereof, that we will be rewarded. You could say it's a "quality of eternal life" issue.

Of those who win the prize of eternal life, not everyone will receive the same glory. Your particular reward will match your individual merit. Christ makes this clear throughout the Gospels. It is thus in our best interest to live out the Good News to the absolute fullest. Just doing the bare minimum for our salvation is a dangerous course; it's some really thin ice. Not only would that put us a hair away from being among the damnable lukewarm, but even if we did attain salvation we would forever have less than what we could have had. If we make it into Paradise, *that* is the most important consideration, bar none. But Christ our God is clearly encouraging us not just to squeak by, but to "lay up for yourselves treasures in heaven" (Mt 6:20).

The Greatest Thanksgiving of All

I saved the very best for last in this book. This is the closest we get in *Heaven Help Us, Now!* to the "solid food" of Christianity, both metaphorically and literally.

If we pay back St. Jude for his great favors to us in the greatest way possible, by following his teachings, then we will come with an open mind and open heart to the pure truth he teaches. This truth he teaches is known as the Gospel of Jesus Christ. The pinnacle and central feature of the Gospel is the thing we know as the "Eucharist." Let me explain.

I am very fond of the old Baltimore Catechism. My dear great-aunt Sr. Mairéad Nic Mhathúna (Margaret McMahon), God rest her soul, and known lovingly to everyone in my family as "Aunt Margie," gave me a copy when I was about eight years old. It was no longer used as a school textbook when I was growing up in the 1980's, but I used it as my primary personal textbook on the Catholic faith. Even as a kid, I did a lot of reading on my own.

The Catechism was laid out in a question and answer format. One of the first questions is, "Where is God?" to which the answer is, "God is everywhere."

Okay. So if the goal is to be united to Jesus Christ, and Christ is God, and God is everywhere, then it shouldn't matter where or how we unite with Him, right?

Wrong.

There are particular times, places, and situations that are more special than others. And there is no time, place, or situation that is more special or holy than when Jesus Christ is *physically* present! During the Catholic Church service known as the Mass, Qurbana, or Divine Liturgy, Jesus Christ *physically, actually, literally* appears in the disguise of what looks like bread and wine. This is the Eucharist. It is the holy of holies. It is Jesus Christ our God who we literally *eat* during Holy Communion, when we consume the Eucharist. It is literal solid food.

It is also metaphorical solid food because the doctrine can be rather tough for a nonbeliever to digest. The Eucharist is so central to Christianity, yet seemingly so difficult to accept that even some people who call themselves Christians reject that it is truly Christ. This includes all Protestants and apparently about two-thirds of nominal Catholics in the United States.[28] Christ, the Lord Himself, faced the exact same disbelief about the Eucharist during His earthly ministry (Jn 6:60-66).

The Eucharist is too big of a topic to give it its due within the scope of this book. However, I would not be doing my duty if I did not at least bring it up. And I must mention that the truth of this dogma is backed up by Eucharistic miracles (look it up!). This is how God works – if He has revealed a truth He also "confirmed the message by the signs that attended it" (Mk 16:20b).

For more on the subject, I recommend the short but deeply informative *Secrets of the Eucharist* by Michael H. Brown. Further, I suggest looking up "Carlo Acutis." I won't spoil it for you, but I'm confident people at every level of faith would be intrigued by the saintly young man's Eucharistic story.

The Eucharist is supremely relevant to the St. Jude Thaddeus devotion. Recall that in Hebrew, Jude/Judas/Judah means "Thanksgiving." Do you know what Eucharist means in Greek? You got it right, "Thanksgiving." Let's let that sink in.

It is as if God uses the human "Thanksgiving" – St. Jude – to get our attention by allowing us to experience the ecstasy of getting out of a hopeless jam. This in turn draws us closer to the "Thanksgiving" who is both human and divine – Jesus Christ, the Eucharist, our God. And then, after uniting ourselves with Him in a definitive manner when we pass from this life, we will experience ecstasy with Him without end.

So, I encourage everybody to have Masses said in thanksgiving for St. Jude's favors to us. It is easy to do – just get in touch with a shrine devoted to Jude Thaddeus. Look over the list of shrines and contact info in Chapter 4, though I caution you always to do your research to make sure you have the most current information.

Also, I encourage everybody to do everything possible to receive the Eucharist worthily, to eat the flesh and drink the blood of the living Jesus Christ without judgement or condemnation. This means coming into the Catholic Church if you are not already in. If you are in the Church already, you must be in a state of grace to receive. That is, you must be free of mortal sin. A good sacramental Confession will take care of that.

Ultimately, all our prayers end up with God and are answered by God. His goodness to us will leave us shocked when we find out the full extent of it in the next life. We could take a cue from St. Jude's friend, and protector during his life on earth, St. Michael the Archangel. In Hebrew, "Michael" means, "Who is like God?" His name is a question which implies its own answer: Nobody and nothing even comes close.

The Lord's goodness is most clearly plain and tangible to us when we experience salvation. The big reward will have to wait for the next life, but we can get glimpses of it in this life. This is St. Jude Thaddeus' biggest contribution to our lives, that his work on our behalf allows us to experience a bit of what salvation feels like, to "taste and see that the LORD is good!" (Ps 34(33):8). It is so good that once we get a taste, it only makes sense to move heaven and Earth to get more.

The end result of our petitions will be joy, because if we stick by Him, He will stick by us. And when we get that ecstatic joy, "Then my soul shall rejoice in the LORD, / exulting in his deliverance. / All my bones shall say [like the Archangel Michael], / 'O LORD, who is like you, / who deliver the weak, / from him who is too strong for him, / the weak and the needy from him who despoils him?'" (Ps 35(34):9-10).

Even if nobody in the world is on our side, all of eternity is rooting for us when we turn to St. Jude Thaddeus in confident prayer. We will be saved, we will be victorious, and our earthly thanksgiving will seamlessly blend into an eternal one (Ps 35(34):27): "Let those who desire my vindication / shout for joy and be glad, / and say evermore, / 'Great is the LORD, / who delights in the welfare of his servant!'"

FINAL BLESSING

Well, that's it for now. My earnest prayer is that anyone who has read *Heaven Help Us, Now!* has gained something positive from it and that it will have been to the profit of the reader's soul. And so, dear reader, I would like to express my personal gratitude to you for allowing me to share this useful knowledge. My deepest thanks to everybody who has accompanied me on this short journey through the key points of the St. Jude Thaddeus devotion. I encourage you to keep on the lookout for my more comprehensive works on God's own first responder, under the forthcoming series title **HEAVEN'S 9-1-1**.

Now that we have truly come to the end of this little book about God's emergency service saint, I think it would be appropriate to close out with the same words with which he concluded his biblical epistle:

Now to him who is able to keep you from falling and to present you without blemish before the presence of his glory with rejoicing, to the only God, our Savior through Jesus Christ our Lord, be glory, majesty, dominion, and authority, before all time and now and for ever. Amen.

APPENDIX A
The Catholic Epistle of St. Jude The Apostle

It is impossible to gain a full appreciation of the St. Jude Thaddeus devotion without being familiar with his apostolic teachings as preserved in the Bible. As such, I have included his epistle here in this appendix, along with a bit of useful and necessary commentary. I believe that *Heaven Help Us, Now!* is unique in presenting three major Catholic translations in sequence after each of the five section headings. Rather than choosing to favor one translation over another, I determined it would be best for you, dear reader, to be presented with legitimate options in order to compare and contrast. I believe this puts you in a better position to glean the word of God from the sacred text if you are not reading it in the original language. I do this myself in my own Bible reading.

Revised Standard Version, Second Catholic Edition

For scriptural references in the main body of *Heaven Help Us, Now!*, I use the Revised Standard Version, Second Catholic Edition, because it seems to be the most popular Bible translation used in the published works of today's faithful English language Catholic writers, such as Scott Hahn and Taylor Marshall.

The Revised Standard Version (RSV) was first published in 1952. It first popped up on my mental radar when I was looking up Catholic resources for the Scottish Gaelic language some years back. The now defunct website of Canan Iain Mac a' Bhreatannaich (Canon John Galbraith, eternal memory) said that the closest equivalent in English to the Gaelic Bible was the RSV. Since Gaelic (of the Donegal, Ireland dialect) happens to be my language at home, this is a matter of note to me.

The Introduction to the RSV's Catholic Edition lauds the translation as one "which combines accuracy and clarity of meaning with beauty of language and traditional diction." It has been accepted by Catholics, Protestants, and Eastern Orthodox alike. The renowned biblical scholar Bruce Metzger, who was on the translation team for the RSV, says that it is the first truly ecumenical edition of the Bible in the English language.[29]

New American Bible, Revised New Testament

The second version of the scriptures given here is the Revised New Testament of the New American Bible (NAB). The original NAB was published in 1970 and was the result of an ambitious project to create the first American Catholic version of the Bible translated from the original languages. Unfortunately, its New Testament had numerous problematic renderings.[30] So, the Catholic Biblical Association of America went back to the drawing board.

The result was published in 1986. It garnered praise for abiding by its primary aim, which was, "to produce a version as accurate and faithful to the meaning of the Greek original as is possible for a translation."[31] The revisers succeeded, according to Metzger, in repairing the inaccuracies and inconsistencies of the 1970 version and producing a final product which was "a substantial improvement over the previous edition."[32]

From 1998 on, it became the standard New Testament text in the United States for the Catholic Lectionary for Mass. Its best feature is arguably its extensive footnotes; these are faithfully Orthodox, magnificently scholarly, and delightfully edifying.

Douay-Rheims

The third translation here, but the first in chronological terms, is the revered Douay-Rheims (D-R). It is the oldest post-Reformation Catholic version of the Bible in the English language, completed in 1582. The D-R was not translated directly from the original languages but through the medium of the Latin Vulgate, which it followed with great precision.

It exercised a tremendous influence on the King James Version (KJV) of 1611, "transmitting to it not only an extensive vocabulary, but also numerous distinct phrases and terms of expression."[33] While the KJV has never been accepted by the Church – King James I of England was a heretic – it is the most influential translation in the history of the English tongue. It had an incalculable impact on the English language itself, so that the Douay-Rheims can rightfully claim to have left its mark on the anglophone world through it.

Despite its influence, the original D-R was difficult for the average English reader to understand, even in its time. It was densely suffused with obscure Latinate terminology – gems such as "parasceve," "scenopegia," "exinanited," and "coiquination." To address this issue, the learned English bishop Richard Challoner spent many years – from 1738 to 1772 – in revising it. The Challoner revision is the version of the D-R most commonly available today, and is still the favored translation of many of today's English-speaking faithful.

A. INTRODUCTION

In this first part of the letter, St. Jude introduces himself to his audience and also blesses them. The blessing is not rhetorical flourish, but a true blessing from the Apostle on all of us who read and study his sacred writing. He goes on to lay out the theme of his epistle – the exhortation to his readers to "contend for the faith," the faith, the unchangeable and final revelation given by Jesus Christ to His Apostles. Jude then introduces the group who are endangering the eternal fate of his beloved sheep – intruders who entered secretly into the Church and who teach a false gospel, a perversion of the truth.

Revised Standard Version:
[1]Jude, a servant of Jesus Christ and brother of James,
To those who are called, beloved in God the Father and kept for Jesus Christ: [2]May mercy, peace, and love be multiplied to you. [3]Beloved, being very eager to write to you of our common salvation, I found it necessary to write appealing to you to contend for the faith which was once for all delivered to the saints. [4]For admission has been secretly gained by some who long ago were designated for this condemnation, ungodly persons who pervert the grace of our God into licentiousness and deny our only Master and Lord, Jesus Christ.

New American Bible:
[1]Jude, a slave of Jesus Christ and brother of James, to those who are called, beloved in God the Father and kept safe for Jesus Christ: [2]may mercy, peace, and love be yours in abundance. [3]Beloved, although I was making every effort to write to you about our common salvation, I now feel a need to write to encourage you to contend for the faith that was once for all handed down to the holy ones. [4]For there have been some

intruders, who long ago were designated for this condemnation, godless persons, who pervert the grace of our God into licentiousness and who deny our only Master and Lord, Jesus Christ.

Douay-Rheims:

¹JUDE, the servant of Jesus Christ, and brother of James: to them that are beloved in God the Father, and preserved in Jesus Christ, and called. ²Mercy unto you, and peace, and charity be fulfilled. ³Dearly beloved, taking all care to write unto you concerning your common salvation, I was under a necessity to write unto you: to beseech you to contend earnestly for the faith once delivered to the saints. ⁴For certain men are secretly entered in (who were written of long ago unto this judgement,) ungodly men, turning the grace of our Lord God into riotousness, and denying the only sovereign Ruler, and our Lord Jesus Christ.

B. ST. JUDE TEACHES FROM THE BIBLE I

This section and the next two cover verses 5-19, St. Jude's extended polemic (an impassioned rhetorical attack) on enemies of the Church who have infiltrated as members of the Church. This polemic is not the main point; it is the extended buildup to the main message in the final section. It is the latter verses which contain the real meat of the Apostle's teaching on how to fight for the faith.

However, verses 5-19 give the necessary background to understanding the final verses, in a manner similar to how the far larger Old Testament is essential for making sense of the New Testament. In them St. Jude uses his divine inspiration to reveal the true nature of the intruders, the wolves in sheep's clothing, and he comforts the faithful by demonstrating that God has already accounted for everything.

We can and should apply the lessons of the intruders here to contemporary events. Jude the Apostle's writing on the crisis he faced was not put in the Bible by God just so we could have arcane historical knowledge. He put it there to guide all Christians for all time, including us in our own circumstances.

Revised Standard Version:

⁵Now I desire to remind you, though you were once for all fully informed, that he who saved a people out of the land of Egypt, afterward destroyed those who did not believe. ⁶And the angels that did not keep their own position but left their proper dwelling have been kept by him in eternal chains in the deepest darkness until the judgement of the great day. ⁷just as Sodom and Gomor'rah and the surrounding cities, which likewise acted immorally and indulged in unnatural lust, serve as an example by undergoing a punishment of eternal fire.

New American Bible:

⁵I wish to remind you, although you know all things, that [the] Lord who once saved a people from the land of Egypt later destroyed those who did not believe. ⁶The angels too, who did not keep to their own domain but deserted their proper dwelling, he has kept in eternal chains, in gloom, for the judgement of the great day. ⁷Likewise, Sodom, Gomorrah, and the surrounding towns, which, in the same manner as they, indulged in sexual promiscuity and practiced unnatural vice, serve as an example by undergoing a punishment of eternal fire.

Douay-Rheims:

⁵I will therefore admonish you, though ye once knew all things, that Jesus, having saved the people out of the land of Egypt, did afterwards destroyed them that believed not: ⁶And the angels who kept not their prin-

cipality, but forsook their own habitation, he hath reserved under darkness in everlasting chains, unto the judgement of the great day. ⁷As Sodom and Gomorrha, and the neighboring cities, in like manner, having given themselves to fornication, and going after other flesh, were made an example, suffering the punishment of eternal fire.

C. ST. JUDE TEACHES FROM THE BIBLE II

"Woe to them!" With this short, clear exclamation, St. Jude epitomizes this section of his epistle. He gives a second set of three Old Testament types against which to compare the intruders who threaten the Christian community. This is followed by his commentary linking the infiltrators to the scriptural references in v. 12. Whereas the previous section called out the heterodox intruders for their personal immorality, this one brands them as teachers who are particularly repugnant because they spread their false ideas to the detriment of the faithful.

A unique highlight of these verses is that St. Jude's special relationship with St. Michael is put on display. In v. 9 he bestows the title "archangel" on Michael, the only time in the Bible he is so titled, and one of only two times the word is used in scripture (the other appearance of it is 1 Thes 4:16). The appellation stuck, and "archangel" is what we call the grand prince of angels to the present day.

Revised Standard Version:

⁸Yet in like manner these men in their dreamings defile the flesh, reject authority, and revile the glorious ones. ⁹But when the archangel Michael, contending with the devil, disputed about the body of Moses, he did not presume to pronounce a reviling judgement upon him, but said, "The Lord rebuke you." ¹⁰But these men revile what they do not understand, and by those things that they know by instinct as irrational animals do,

they are destroyed. [11]Woe to them! For they walk in the way of Cain, and abandon themselves for the sake of gain to Balaam's error, and perish in Ko'rah's rebellion. [12]These are blemishes on your love feasts, as they boldly carouse together, looking after themselves; waterless clouds, carried along by winds; fruitless trees in autumn, twice dead, uprooted; [13]wild waves of the sea, casting up the foam of their own shame; wandering stars for whom the deepest darkness has been reserved forever.

New American Bible:

[8]Similarly, these dreamers nevertheless also defile the flesh, scorn leadership, and revile glorious beings. [9]Yet the archangel Michael, when he argued with the devil in a dispute over the body of Moses, did not venture to pronounce a reviling judgement upon him but said, "May the Lord rebuke you!" [10]But these people revile what they do not understand and are destroyed by what they know by nature like irrational animals. [11]Woe to them! They followed in the way of Cain, abandoned themselves to Balaam's error for the sake of gain, and perished in the rebellion of Korah. [12]These are blemishes on your love feasts, as they carouse fearlessly and look after themselves. They are waterless clouds blown about by winds, fruitless trees in late autumn, twice dead and uprooted. [13]They are like wild waves of the sea, foaming up their shameless deeds, wandering stars for whom the gloom of darkness has been reserved forever.

Douay-Rheims:

[8]In like manner these men also defile the flesh, and despise dominion, and blaspheme majesty. [9]When Michael the archangel, disputing with the devil, contended about the body of Moses, he durst not bring against him the judgement of railing speech, but said: The Lord command thee. [10]But these men blaspheme whatever things they know not: and what

things soever they naturally know, like dumb beasts, in these they are corrupted. [11]Woe unto them, for they have gone in the way of Cain: and after the error of Balaam they have for reward poured out themselves, and have perished in the contradiction of Core. [12]These are spots in their banquets, feasting together without fear, feeding themselves, clouds without water, which are carried about by winds, trees of the autumn, unfruitful, twice dead, plucked up by the roots, [13]Raging waves of the sea, foaming out their own confusion; wandering stars, to whom the storm of darkness is reserved for ever.

D. ST. JUDE TEACHES FROM PROPHECY

In this section, the Apostle concludes his polemic against the infiltration of the Church with an ancient prophecy and a more recent one. (Both prophecies are ancient from our point of view!). He follows the same format as the previous two sections, first giving the reference and then following it with commentary and interpretation. His purpose is to console the faithful by demonstrating that both their difficulties and the just judgement of the troublemakers were foretold. The Christian who internalizes this message can smile with existential peace. Don't worry, everything will be alright.

Revised Standard Version:

[14]It was of these also that Enoch in the seventh generation from Adam prophesied, saying, "Behold, the Lord came with myriads of his holy ones, [15]to execute judgement on all and to convict all the ungodly of all their deeds of ungodliness which they have committed in such an ungodly way, and of all the harsh things which ungodly sinners have spoken against him." [16]These are grumblers, malcontents, following their own passions, loud-mouthed boasters, flattering people to gain advantage. [17]But you must remember, beloved, the predictions of the apos-

tles of our Lord Jesus Christ; [18]they said to you, "In the last time there will be scoffers, following their own ungodly passions." [19]It is these who set up divisions, worldly people, devoid of the Spirit.

New American Bible:

[14]Enoch, of the seventh generation from Adam, prophesied also about them when he said, "Behold, the Lord has come with his countless holy ones [15]to execute judgement on all and to convict everyone for all the godless deeds that they committed and for all the harsh words godless sinners have uttered against him." [16]These people are complainers, disgruntled ones who live by their desires; their mouths utter bombast as they fawn over people to gain advantage. [17]But you, beloved, remember the words spoken beforehand by the apostles of our Lord Jesus Christ, [18]for they told you, "In [the] last time there will be scoffers who will live according to their own godless desires." [19]These are the ones who cause divisions; they live on the natural plane, devoid of the Spirit.

Douay-Rheims:

[14]Now of these Enoch also, the seventh from Adam, prophesied, saying: Behold, the Lord cometh with thousands of his saints, [15]To execute judgement upon all, and to reprove all the ungodly for all the works of their ungodliness, whereby they have done ungodly, and of all the hard things which ungodly sinners have spoken against God. [16]These are murmurers, full of complaints, walking according to their own desires, and their mouth speaketh proud things, admiring persons for gain's sake. [17]But you, my dearly beloved, be mindful of the words which have been spoken before by the apostles of our Lord Jesus Christ, [18]Who told you, that in the last time there should come mockers, walking according

to their own desires in ungodliness. [19]These are they, who separate themselves, sensual men, having not the Spirit.

E. ST. JUDE'S INSTRUCTIONS FOR YOU

Now comes the part of the Epistle that everything before this has been building up to. These latter verses are where "the real substance of Jude's appeal to his readers," as the biblical scholar Richard Bauckham relates. This is where St. Jude explains what contending or fighting for the faith (v. 3) actually consists of. These are his instructions for you, for me, for all of us whose lives have been so positively and profoundly affected by his powerful prayers on our behalf. Scholars who have taken Jude seriously have noticed that in these final verses, "the brevity of the text contrasts with the richness of the doctrine it contains" (also from Bauckham). Let's take a look.

Revised Standard Version:

[20]But you, beloved, build yourselves up on your most holy faith; pray in the Holy Spirit; [21]keep yourselves in the love of God; wait for the mercy of our Lord Jesus Christ unto eternal life. [22]And convince some, who doubt; [23]save some, by snatching them out of the fire; on some have mercy with fear, hating even the garment spotted by the flesh. [24]Now to him who is able to keep you from falling and to present you without blemish in the presence of his glory with rejoicing, [25]to the only God, our Savior through Jesus Christ our Lord, be glory, majesty, dominion, and authority, before all time and now and forever. Amen.

New American Bible:

[20]But you, beloved, build yourselves up in your most holy faith; pray in the holy Spirit. [21]Keep yourselves in the love of God and wait for the mercy of our Lord Jesus Christ that leads to eternal life. [22]On those who

waiver, have mercy; [23]save others by snatching them out of the fire; on others have mercy with fear, abhorring even the outer garment stained by the flesh. [24]To the one who is able to keep you from stumbling and to present you unblemished and exultant, in the presence of his glory, [25]to the only God, our savior, through Jesus Christ our Lord be glory, majesty, power, and authority from ages past, now, and ages to come. Amen.

Douay-Rheims:

[20]But you, my beloved, building yourselves upon your most holy faith, praying in the Holy Ghost, [21]Keep yourselves in the love of God, waiting for the mercy of our Lord Jesus Christ, unto life everlasting. [22]And some indeed reprove, being judged: [23]But others save, pulling them out of the fire. And on others have mercy, in fear, hating also the spotted garment which is carnal. [24]Now to him who is able to preserve you without sin, and to present you spotless before the presence of his glory with exceeding joy, in the coming of our Lord Jesus Christ, [25]To the only God our Saviour through Jesus Christ our Lord, be glory and magnificence, empire and power, before all ages, and now, and for all ages of ages. Amen.

APPENDIX B
The Basic Christian Prayers

Every single soul who accepts the reality that Jesus is Lord should know at least the first nine of these prayers by heart. They are the foundational prayers of Christianity, and were all given by God to His people, the Church. He gave us the first five directly through the Bible, the next two (6 & 7) through the liturgy of antiquity which was inspired by scripture, and the next two after that (8 & 9) through private revelations in the 20th century.

The last three prayers (10-12) have been around for centuries. They are not as easily traceable back to God Himself as the first nine prayers are, but express pious sentiments that are in accord with the Gospel. As such, they greatly please our Lord, who loves when His creatures unite themselves in one Spirit with Him.

Alternate titles are in parentheses.

FROM DIVINE SOURCES
1. THE SIGN OF THE CROSS

This is the most basic and fundamental prayer of Christianity. When we say it we are saying the exact words given to us by Jesus Christ (Mt 28:19). Ain't it amazing – we are repeating words spoken by God Himself! The words are accompanied by a hand gesture, starting with the fingers of the right hand brought together and then touching the forehead. In the Eastern tradition, the thumb, index finger, and middle finger are brought together in memory of the Three Persons of the Holy

Trinity; the other two fingers are folded into the palm in memory of the two natures of Christ: human and divine.

You next touch your hand to the center of your chest with the words, "and of the Son." Then, you touch both shoulders in succession while saying, "and of the Holy Spirit." In the Byzantine tradition you go from right shoulder to left, and in the Latin tradition you go from left shoulder to right.

In the name of the Father, and of the Son, and of the Holy Spirit. Amen.

2. THE LORD'S PRAYER (OUR FATHER, PATER NOSTER)

When the disciples of the Lord asked Him how to pray, this prayer was the answer He gave them (Lk 11:1-4; Mt 6:9-13). These are words spoken by God the Son and given to us so that we can give them back to God the Father. Talk about full circle! It is simply the most inestimable privilege to be included in the divine life as we make our way back to our Creator, our Father.

The Lord's Prayer is the perfect prayer, the epitome of all Christian prayer. It starts with the introductory address to the Almighty, followed by seven petitions. All other prayers are just wordier and more detailed versions of the petitions of the Lord's Prayer, in the same way that all moral laws are wordier and more detailed versions of the Ten Commandments.

For more introductory information on the Lord's Prayer, see the detailed and authoritative *Catechism of the Catholic Church*, 2759-2865.

Our Father who art in heaven,
¹Hallowed be thy name.
²Thy kingdom come.

³Thy will be done on earth, as it is in heaven.
⁴Give us this day our daily bread,
⁵And forgive us our trespasses, as we forgive those who trespass against us;
⁶And lead us not into temptation,
⁷But deliver us from evil.
Amen.

3. THE JESUS PRAYER

The *Catechism* tells us that "Jesus always responds to a prayer offered in faith: 'Your faith has made you well; go in peace'" (2616). The Jesus Prayer, developed in the Eastern tradition, is the ancient invocation which most succinctly expresses this faith; we believe that the Lord saves. It is sublime in its simplicity. The prayer is directly from the inspired word of God, spliced together from the confession that "Jesus Christ is Lord" (Phil 2:11), the primordial apostolic and papal confessions of Christ's divine Sonship (Mt 14:33, 16:16), and the petitions to the Lord for mercy from the blind beggar (Mk 10:47) and the publican (Lk 18:13). Through the faithful use of the Jesus Prayer "the heart is opened to human wretchedness and the Savior's mercy" (CCC 2667).

For more introductory information, see the *Catechism of the Catholic Church* 2616, 2667-2668.

Lord Jesus Christ, Son of God, have mercy on me, a sinner.

4. THE ANGELIC SALUTATION (HAIL MARY, AVE MARIA)

This classic Christian prayer expresses our eternal gratitude to Mary for cooperating with the Father's will by welcoming His Son into her womb to become her son as well, making the salvation of the human race possible. It starts with the greeting that the Archangel Gabriel gave to the young Mary announcing that she would bear the Messiah (Lk 1:48), thus to become the *Theotokos*, the Mother of God (literally "God-bearer"). The next line is the prophetic welcome greeting of St. Elizabeth to her kinswoman, Mary. Both women were pregnant, Elizabeth with John the Baptist and Mary with *Jesus* (literally "the Lord saves"). The last line was added by the Church in the 16th century, around the time of the Council of Trent. It is without a doubt the best known Marian prayer.

Most non-religious or non-Catholic Americans would be most familiar with this classic prayer from the football play named after its opening words. This reference does have its origins in the pious practices of faithful Notre Dame football players in the early 20th century, though the public understanding of it has been much secularized. If there is any saving grace for such a worldly use of something so sacred, it would be that it bears witness to Mary being our surest route to Jesus when we are in desperate need. St. Jude Thaddeus performs his own mission with the help and support of his heavenly Mother, since they are both on the same grand mission of leading souls to Christ.

For more on the Angelic Salutation and Marian prayer, see the *Catechism of the Catholic Church* 2673-2679, 2682.

Hail Mary, full of grace, the Lord is with thee.
Blessed art thou amongst women, and blessed is the fruit of thy womb, Jesus.
Holy Mary, Mother of God, pray for us sinners, now and at the hour of our death.
Amen.

5. GLORY BE (GLORIA PATRI)

This doxological prayer is built from bricks that come from a few different spots in scripture: the *Gloria* of the angels in Bethlehem (Lk

2:14), the Trinitarian commission of Christ (Mt 28:19-20), and the praise of God's eternity by our own St. Jude (verses 24-25).

The Glory Be exists in a couple of different translations, the one given here is the most commonly encountered.

Glory be to the Father, and to the Son, and to the Holy Spirit, as it was in the beginning, is now, and ever shall be, world without end. Amen.

6. THE THRICE HOLY HYMN (TRISAGION)

This short, ancient hymn praises God the Holy Trinity and begs Him for mercy. It is inspired by the angelic hymns of praise in Isaiah 6:3 and Revelation 4:8, and the pleading for mercy in Psalms 51 and 123.

In the Divine Liturgy (Mass) of the rite of Constantinople, it is chanted after the introductory antiphons and before the Epistle and Gospel readings. I find the Ruthenian melody particularly beautiful.

It is also the final prayer of the popular Chaplet of Divine Mercy.

Holy God, Holy and Mighty, Holy and Immortal, have mercy on us.
(*three times*)

6. THE APOSTLES' CREED

The Apostle's Creed is the most basic summation of what a Christian believes. By tradition, it goes back to the Twelve Apostles themselves, each of whom contributed an article of faith. As we can see, St. Jude Thaddeus contributed the eleventh article, that of belief in "the resurrection of the body." This is truly appropriate and profound, since it was he who safeguarded and transported the premier relic of the Resurrection of the Lord, the object now known as the "Holy Shroud of Turin" and historically as the "Mandylion." It was with this sacred object that he cured King Abgar of Edessa, thus laying the groundwork for his later veneration as the Saint of Hopeless Causes.

In listing the articles of faith along with the Apostles associated with them, I have followed the classic work, *An Teagasg Críosdaidhe* by Bonabhentura Ó hEódhasa, OFM, published in 1611. (Few in the anglophone world might have heard of this book or its author, but it is one of the earliest printed works in the Irish language).

[1]**I believe in God, the Father almighty, creator of heaven and earth.**
Simon Peter
[2]**I believe in Jesus Christ, his only Son, our Lord.** *Andrew*
[3]**He was conceived by the power of the Holy Spirit and born of the Virgin Mary.** *John*
[4]**He suffered under Pontius Pilate, was crucified, died, and was buried.** *James the Greater*
[5]**He descended into hell. On the third day he rose again.** *Thomas*
[6]**He ascended into heaven and is seated at the right hand of the Father.** *James the Less*
[7]**He will come again to judge the living and the dead.** *Philip*
[8]**I believe in the Holy Spirit,** *Nathaniel Bartholomew*
[9]**the holy catholic Church,** *Matthew*
[10]**the communion of saints,** *Simon the Zealot*
[11]**the resurrection of the body,** *Jude Thaddeus*
[12]**and life everlasting.** *Matthias*
Amen.

8. THE FATIMA PRAYER

The Mother of God personally appeared to three children at Fatima in Portugal in 1917. She gave this prayer to them, which one of them wrote down, and requested that it be recited after each mystery of the

Rosary. The version here is taken directly from the account of Sister Lucía, the visionary who wrote down the words of the Virgin Mary.[34]

The apparitions are approved by the Church. Their authenticity was confirmed by the most witnessed public miracle since Moses parted the Red Sea. Fatima's "Miracle of the Sun" was seen by tens of thousands of people, some of whom survived into the 21st century. Sister Lucía herself went to the Lord in 2005 and is now up for canonization as a saint.

O my Jesus, forgive us, save us from the fire of hell. Lead all souls to Heaven, especially those who are most in need.

9. THE DIVINE MERCY

Jesus Christ appeared to a Polish nun named Faustina Kowalska, now St. Faustina, starting in 1931. She died 1938 on the brink of World War II breaking out and her country being overrun by the satanic dictators, Hitler and Stalin. Before our Lord took her, He imparted to her the popular devotion now known as the Divine Mercy. This is the main prayer of the highly popular Chaplet of Divine Mercy. The Holy Spirit spoke to St. Faustina in order that we all might have these words to call upon the Lord's mercy in a manner pleasing to Him. What a tremendous gift!

Eternal Father, I offer You the Body and Blood, Soul and Divinity of Your dearly beloved Son, Our Lord Jesus Christ, in atonement for our sins and those of the whole world; for the sake of His sorrowful Passion, have mercy on us and on the whole world.

PIOUS EXTRAS
10. HAIL, HOLY QUEEN (SALVE REGINA)

This wonderful Marian anthem is strongly associated with the glorious First Crusade, and with St. Bernard of Clairvaux and his Cistercian Order. St. Bernard was not only a loyal and loving son of Mary, but if we recall, he was an exceptionally early western European devotee of St. Jude (he lived in the 12ᵗʰ century).

The Salve Regina traditionally concludes the Rosary.

Hail, Holy Queen, Mother of Mercy, our life, our sweetness, and our hope!
To thee do we cry, poor banished children of Eve. To thee do we send up our sighs, mourning and weeping in this valley of tears.
Turn, then, most gracious Advocate, thine eyes of mercy toward us, and after this, our exile, show unto us the blessed fruit of thy womb, Jesus.
O clement, O loving, O sweet Virgin Mary!

Pray for us, O holy Mother of God, that we may be made worthy of the promises of Christ.

All of the previous ten prayers are combined in different arrangements in various popular devotions, the two most well known of which are the Rosary of the Blessed Virgin Mary and the Chaplet of Divine Mercy. The Jesus Prayer can also be prayed iteratively on Rosary beads.

To learn how to say the longer devotions, a simple internet search, "how to pray the rosary," etc., will get you going. It is well worth the effort to save your soul from damnation. (Yes, I really just said that! "The fear of the LORD is the beginning of wisdom" (Prv 9:10)). Here are some good, engaging books on these devotions: *The Secret of the Ro-*

sary by St. Louis de Montfort; *The Divine Mercy Message and Devotion* by Fr. Seraphim Michalenko; and *The Jesus Prayer: A Cry for Mercy, a Path of Renewal* by John Michael Talbot.

11. MEMORARE

This one is a personal favorite of mine. It is the loving pleading of a child to his or her heavenly Mother. I first learned it from my grandmother, Síne Nic Mhathúna Uí Fhianghusa (Jean McMahon Fennessy), simply "Nana" to her grandkids. She would always pray it when getting in the car to go anywhere, whether she was the driver or not.

I use it frequently, for any number of needs. The Mother of God has in turn astounded me any number of times with her manifest intercession. It thus shares a similarity of focus with the St. Jude devotion, and makes for an excellent partner to any of the Jude Thaddeus prayers. It is consequently quite fitting that the Memorare is the eleventh prayer listed here, since St. Jude is usually listed as the eleventh Apostle.

The Memorare probably dates back at least to the late 16th century, and was extracted from a longer Latin prayer of the 15th century.

Remember, O most gracious Virgin Mary, that never was it known that anyone who fled to thy protection, implored thy help, or sought thy intercession was left unaided.

Inspired with this confidence, I fly unto thee, O Virgin of virgins, my Mother; to thee to I come; before thee I stand, sinful and sorrowful.

O Mother of the Word Incarnate, despise not my petitions, but in thy mercy hear and answer them. Amen.

12. A PRAYER FOR GOVERNMENT

This prayer was composed in 1791 by John Carroll, the first bishop and archbishop of the United States, and was distributed to all the Catholic parishes of the nation. Archbishop Carroll was the cousin of Charles Carroll of Carrollton, who was the longest surviving signer of the Declaration of Independence, the only Catholic signer, and the first "richest man in America" (a distinction later held by the likes of John Rockefeller, Bill Gates, and Jeff Bezos). The Carroll family of Maryland – "Carroll" is the anglicized form of the Irish *Ó Cearúill* – were descended from the rulers of Éile, a small kingdom in south central Ireland. By their staunch support for American independence they were able to help win the new nation's freedom from the satanic tyranny of England, a blessing that was denied to the land of their ancestry.

The Carrolls were instrumental on the ecclesiastical side of things, too; they set up the fledgling Church in America on a strong footing. The petitions of this prayer are a distillation of true Christian hope for the new republic. The words can certainly be adapted to your own national circumstances if you happen to live outside the U.S. because the principles are universal (though prayers for the U.S. are still much appreciated even if you're not American!).

Archbishop Carroll's Prayer for Government is doubtlessly the least known of the prayers I have listed in this appendix. It thus shares a similarity with St. Matthias, one of the least known of the Twelve Apostles and whose most well-known claim to fame is being the last Apostle chosen. Matthias does not even appear in the Gospels, only coming on the scene at the beginning of the Acts of the Apostles.

I certainly hope to make this prayer a little less obscure. I only discovered its existence fairly recently while reading Timothy Gordon's *Catholic Republic: Why America Will Perish Without Rome*. I have since incorporated it into the petitions of my daily Rosary, and its themes could not be more fitting for our times. I highly encourage every Christian to do the same.

We pray Thee, O God of might, wisdom, and justice, through whom authority is rightly administered, laws are enacted, and judgement decreed, assist with Thy Holy Spirit of counsel and fortitude the President of these United States, that his administration may be conducted in righteousness, and be eminently useful to Thy people over whom he presides; by encouraging due respect for virtue and religion; by a faithful execution of the laws in justice and mercy; and by restraining vice and immorality. Let the light of Thy divine wisdom direct the deliberations of Congress, and shine forth in all the proceedings and laws framed for our rule and government, so that they may tend to the preservation of peace, the promotion of national happiness, the increase of industry, sobriety, and useful knowledge; and may perpetuate to us the blessing of equal liberty. Amen.

Notes

If a source listed in these Notes also appears in the Select Bibliography, only last name (or keyword) and page number (if relevant) are given here. Otherwise, the full citation is given.

1. "Apostolic Constitution *Fidei Depositum.*" *Catechism of the Catholic Church*, p. 3.
2. "Apostolic Constitution…" p. 5.
3. "Dogmatic Constitution on Divine Revelation," chp. 2. *St. Joseph Edition of the New American Bible.*
4. Saint-Omer, p. 69.
5. "How Many People Have Ever Lived on Earth?" *prb.org*, January 2020.
6. Morgan, p. 101.
7. Fox, Robin. *The Tory Islanders: A People of the Celtic Fringe.* Cambridge University Press, 1978, p. 150.
8. Orsi, p. 104.
9. Martin, Michelle. "Meet Dominican Friar Who Takes Care of St. Jude Relic." *Chicago Catholic*, 25 June 2017.
10. Finley, p. 101.
11. Orsi, pp. 208-9.
12. Di Genua et al., p. 3.
13. Spilman, pp. 110-11.
14. Orsi, p. 208.
15. Malone, pp. 25-26.
16. Thorman, p. 23.
17. Pope Benedict XVI, p. 112.

18. Morgan, p. 23.

19. Stenhouse.

20. Orsi, p. 142.

21. Thorman, p. 23.

22. Mershman, Francis. "Litany." *The Catholic Encyclopedia*. Vol. 9. New York: Robert Appleton Company, 1910. Newadvent.org.

23. Orsi, p. 114.

24. "Thank You St. Jude!" Atonementfriars.org/st-jude-prayer-circle/. Accessed 14 February 2020.

25. Bauckham, p. 285.

26. Potts, Robert. "The Poet at Play." *The Guardian*, 11 May 2001.

27. Michalenko and Flynn, pp. 70-71.

28. Eli, Bradley. "Poll: 7 in 10 US Catholics Don't Believe in Real Presence." *ChurchMilitant.com*, 6 August 2019.

29. Metzger, pp. 122, 161.

30. Metzger, p. 129.

31. Metzger, p. 152.

32. Metzger, p. 153.

33. Metzger, p. 68.

34. *Fatima*, p. 179.

Select Bibliography

The Major Sources

Catechism of the Catholic Church. Libreria Editice Vaticana, 1994.

The Holy Bible: Douay-Rheims Version. New Testament, 1582. Old Testament, 1609, 1610. Challoner revision, 1752. Saint Benedict Press and TAN Books, 2009.

The Holy Bible: Revised Standard Version, Second Catholic Edition. Ignatius Press, 2006.

St. Joseph Edition of the New American Bible: Including the Revised New Testament and the Revised Psalms. Catholic Book Publishing Corp., 1992.

Everyone Else

Most of the works listed below are books, some are articles or websites. Many of these are wonderfully Orthodox sources. Others, however, are not written from a faith-based perspective. So fair WARNING: A work being placed on this list does not indicate that I necessarily agree with all the opinions expressed in it!

However, they are all informative and valuable in one way or another.

I have included the original publication year for older works (those which first came out prior to the mid-20th century).

A Catechism of Christian Doctrine: Prepared and Enjoined by the Third Plenary Council of Baltimore. Benziger Brothers, 1885.

Bauckham, Richard. *Jude and the Relatives of Jesus in the Early Church*. T & T Clark, 2004.

Brown, Michael H. *Secrets of the Eucharist.* Queenship Publishing Co., 2000.

Chesterton, G. K. *Orthodoxy.* 1908. Ignatius, 1995.

De Monfort, Louis. *The Secret of the Rosary.* 1710. TAN Books, 1987.

Di Genua, Andrea, Emanuela Marinelli, Ivan Polverari, and Domenico Repice. "Judas, Thaddeus, Addai: possible connections with the vicissitudes of the Edessan and Constantinopolitan Mandylion and any research perspectives." *Workshop on Advances in the Turin Shroud Investigation (ATSI),* 4–5 September 2014. Academia.edu.

Fatima in Lucia's Own Words. Edited by Louis Kondor. Secretariado dos Pastorinhos, 2002.

Finley, Mitch. *Saint Anthony and Saint Jude: True Stories of Heavenly Help.* Liguori Publications, 2001.

Gordon, Timothy. *Catholic Republic: Why America Will Perish Without Rome.* Sophia Institute Press, Crisis Publications, 2019.

Malone, Dandridge M. *Small Unit Leadership: A Commonsense Approach.* Presidio Press, 1983.

"Menaion." *Metropolitan Cantor Institute.* Byzantine Catholic Archeparchy of Pittsburg, Mci.archpitt.org/liturgy/Menaion.

Metzger, Bruce M. *The Bible in Translation: Ancient and English Versions.* Baker Academic, 2001.

Michalenko, Seraphim, with Vinny Flynn and Robert A. Stackpole. *The Divine Mercy Message and Devotion.* Marian Press, 2005.

Missick, Stephen Andrew. *The Saint Jude Thaddeus Storybook.* 2020.

Morgan, Brian. *The Saint of the Impossible: Everything You Wanted to Know About Saint Jude.* The Writers Trust, 2014.

Ó hEodhasa Bonabhentura. *An Teagasg Críosdaidhe.* Irish Franciscan College of St. Anthony's, 1611. Edited by Fearghal Mac Raghnaill, Dublin Institute of Advanced Studies, 1976.

Orsi, Robert A. *Thank You St. Jude: Women's Devotion to the Patron Saint of Hopeless Causes.* Yale University Press, 1996.

Pope Benedict XVI. *The Apostles and Their Co-Workers.* Our Sunday Visitor, 1997.

Publican's Prayer Book. 3rd ed., Sophia Press, 2017.

Romero, Jesse. *The Devil in the City of Angels: My Encounters with the Diabolical.* TAN Books, 2019.

Ruffin, C. Bernard. *The Twelve: The Lives of the Apostles After Calvary.* Our Sunday Visitor, 1997.

Spilman, Frances. *The Twelve: Lives and Legends of the Apostles.* The Goldhead Group, 2017.

St. Jude Thaddeus: Devotional Exercises and Novena Prayers. Dominican Fathers, 1942.

Saint-Omer, Edward. *St. Gerard Majella: The Wonder-Worker and Patron of Expectant Mothers.* Mission Church Press, 1907. TAN Books, 1999.

Talbot, John Michael. *The Jesus Prayer: A Cry for Mercy, a Path of Renewal.* IVP Books, 2019.

Thorman, Donald J. *St. Jude, Saint of the Impossible.* Ave Maria Press, 1958.